LISTENOLOGY
FOR KIDS

Elaine Heney

"We begin by listening to the horse"

Elaine Heney

All rights reserved. No part of this publication may be reproduced, distributed, or transmitted in any form or by any means, including photocopying, recording, or other electronic or mechanical methods, without the prior written permission of the publisher. Copyright © 2022 Elaine Heney. Edited by Kas Fitzpatrick. Printer: Ingram Publisher Services UK 1 Deltic Avenue, Rooksley Milton Keynes, MK13 8LD, United Kingdom. Publisher & EU authorised representative: Elaine Heney, Design Font Apps Ltd, St. Galls House, St. Gall Gardens South, Milltown, Dublin 14, Ireland. www.elaineheneybooks.com This book has been designed and manufactured in accordance with the general safety requirement laid down in Article 5, GPSR. ISBN printed on back cover.

THIS BOOK
BELONGS TO

Children's books by Elaine Heney
www.elaineheneybooks.com

Horse Care for Kids
Listenology for Kids
P is for PONY

The Forgotten Horse
The Show Horse
The Mayfield Horse
The Stolen Horse
The Adventure Horse
The Lost Horse

The Riding School Connemara Pony
The Storm and the Connemara Pony
The Surprise Puppy and the Connemara Pony
The Castle Charity Ride and the Connemara Pony
The Shipwreck and the Connemara Pony
The Christmas Connemara Pony

Saddlestone | Sinead & Strawberry
Saddlestone | Roisin & Rhubarb
Saddlestone | Conor & Coconut
Saddlestone | Fiona & Foxtrot
Saddlestone | Quiz book

Horse books by Elaine Heney

Equine Listenology Guide
Dressage for Beginners
Listenology Guide to Bitless Bridles
151 Polework Exercises for Horses
The Galway Connemara

TABLE OF CONTENTS

A horse's best friend
The nature of horses
Horse communication
The herd leader
Building a bond
Horse breeds
Horse colours
Buying a horse
Horse anatomy
Equine skeleton
The hoof
Your horse's teeth
Age of physical maturity
Horse people
Where horses live
Horse care
Horse food
Poisonous plants

Sick horses
Grooming your horse
Horse rugs
Saddles & bridles
How to fit a bridle
Riding bitless
How to fit a saddle
Taking care of your tack
Horse safety
Groundwork exercises
Walking in hand
Riding horses
Polework exercises
Feel, balance & timing
Riding skills
Collection
Shoulder in & out
Good horsemanship

A HORSE'S BEST FRIEND

Being around horses is an amazing experience. Many people fall in love with horses when they are very young, then they carry on loving them for their whole lives. When we are around horses we can have so much fun!

We can also meet new friends and learn lots of new things, sometimes changing our lives forever.

Horses are a lot more than learning to walk, trot & canter. Horses can also work on the farm, pull a cart, compete at shows, become a police horse and help people to learn important life skills. But our connection to horses goes far beyond all of these activities too.

With horses we can create amazing partnerships. Partnerships where we understand what our horse is thinking and they understand our thoughts too. A horse is often a much loved family member who we adore. Every horse deserves to be cherished and loved, no matter what age they are, what breed or what colour their coat is.

"It all begins by listening to the horse"

We have a unique opportunity to build trust & connection with each horse we meet! And just like people, each horse is different and unique with their own characteristics & quirks - just like us! We respect each horse and treat them as very intelligent, sensitive creatures. And we always do our best to see the world from the horse's perspective, by listening to the horse.

But here is the unusual thing - loving horses and being their best friend isn't all about riding! In fact, it's about being part of our horse's lives - even when they are just in the field. This includes young horses under four or five who have not yet been started, horses who cannot be ridden for any reason, and older retired horses.

I hope you enjoy reading this book. You may have a horse of your own. Or perhaps you spend time at a riding school or with other people's horses. And if you don't have a chance to be around them at the moment but you just love them anyway - this book is for you too.

Elaine Heney.

THE NATURE OF HORSES

Horses aren't machines like a car or a motorcycle. Horses are like us really. They have feelings and they have good days and bad days. Sometimes they get tired and sometimes they are bursting with energy. Every horse is unique. They all have their own personalities. Some horses can be quiet and some more outgoing. Some horses take things slowly and others seem to do everything at a hundred miles an hour.

BECOME A GREAT TEACHER

One common mistake to avoid is to think that you can treat every horse the same - and it will work for all of them. When you're at school your teacher doesn't treat everyone the same. **They take the time to help everyone differently depending on what they need.**

It's the same with horses.

We have to look at the horse in front of us and take the time to work out what they need, what will be best for them.

SMART HORSES

It's easy for us humans to misunderstand what our horses are telling us. And unfortunately this can lead to us thinking that they are being naughty or that they mean to upset us. That's not how they work at all! Horses might do things we don't want them to do, or that frustrate us, but they are just "horses being horses". They don't make plans to do things to upset us. They just don't think like that.

HORSE BODY LANGUAGE

Horses are very clever at just being horses. They are very clever at making themselves understood to other horses, so we need to learn to understand how they do that. Horses communicate mostly by body language, sometimes in very tiny ways that we don't even notice unless we look carefully.

Horses mean something when they move towards another horse or if they push it away. *They aren't being mean.* They want something to happen and they are seeing if the other horse will cooperate.

HORSE COMMUNICATION

A horse might want to get to eat hay in a feeder but another horse is in the way. If they are confident, they will approach and send signals to the other horse for it to move to let them get to the feeder. What happens next means something to both horses - it tells them who is the one in charge. Either the horse at the feeder will move and let the other in, or it will refuse to move, maybe give a "go away" look, or threaten to bite or kick.

A hay feeder with room for multiple horses.

Sometimes the signals horses give are really small, like a flick of an ear, a swish of the tail, lifting a leg or yawning The more time we spend with them the more we will notice these things and start to understand what they mean.

THE HERD LEADER

People talk about a group of horses having a "herd leader". The herd leader isn't necessarily the horse who seems to be in charge - because the other horses get out of their way. The herd leader is the horse who the others look to when they are worried. It is the horse they follow if they feel that they need to run away. It might well be a horse who is kind to others and is easy for them to be around.

Horses will sometimes bite and kick each other, or buck towards another horse. They aren't being mean. It's just how they talk to each other. If you watch you will see that before they make a big move like a bite they will give little signals first - like for example swishing their tail, pulling a face, and putting their ears back. Other horses are very good at seeing and understanding these signs, but sometimes we humans miss them completely.

HOW HORSES TALK TO US

Horses know that we are not horses - but that doesn't stop them sometimes using their horse-talk to try to tell us what they want us to do or how they feel. The more we learn about horses the more we get to notice when this happens and to know what to do.

I use body language!

IS YOUR HORSE PUSHING YOU AROUND?

The number one miscommunication I see often is horses pushing people around who don't realise it's happening. Have a look for yourself when you are around people with horses. *How many of the horses are walking into their people and pushing the person to make them step back?*

Wouldn't life be nicer for both of them, if the person knew how to gently ask the horse not to do that, and to give them some personal space? *This is not the horse's fault.* The human has forgotten to teach them the fundamentals of personal space.

Personal space is very important. No one likes getting their toes stepped on!

GIVE YOUR HORSE TIME TO UNDERSTAND

Sometimes a horse is telling us that they don't want anything to happen. Instead they need a bit of time to think or rest. They might lick their lips, yawn, drop their head, even shut their eyes - these things give us a clue that it might be time to give them a little break.

Us humans like to feel cared for, and we like to have a lovely hug when we are tired. Sometimes horses just want us to step back and leave them alone for a little while. They don't always need a cuddle or a stroke.

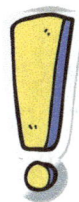

YOU KNOW WHAT'S REALLY CLEVER ABOUT HORSES? THEY ACTUALLY MANAGE TO UNDERSTAND US!

They are very aware of how we move our bodies, our tone of voice, whether we are relaxed or tense, happy or angry. Sometimes we give them confusing signals. Like for example wanting to get on and ride, but feeling a bit scared about actually getting on. Or asking them to go forward while holding tight on the reins so they can't go forwards. No wonder horses sometimes get confused about what we want from them!

You will recognise what your horse is trying to tell you from the signals that he gives. We're often taught that a horse putting their ears back means that they aren't happy and maybe feeling aggressive. This can be true - if a horse pins their ears right back, wrinkles their nose, and has an unhappy expression then you are right to wonder what is causing it and be careful around them.

Horses will also put their ears back when they are relaxed, but you can tell the difference by the expression on their face and how they are holding the rest of their body. Sometimes you will see a horse with its ears back while being ridden. The unhappy horse will also look tense all over and have a tense look on its face. But if the horse is relaxed and has a soft look in its eye, those ears tell you that it is listening to the rider and concentrating.

Horses sometimes give us a very clear warning with their hind legs. If a horse is looking tense and unhappy at the front end, then they might also be lifting a hind leg and warning us that they might kick. Any time you see something like this and you're not sure if you are safe, find an adult to help.

HOW TO BUILD A BOND

You can build a great bond with your horse. Many things will help with this, starting by being calm and patient and treating your horse kindly. Use a gentle voice around them, never shout, and use your voice to praise them for doing good things.

With horses "actions speak louder than words". They like us to be calm and patient and to use a kind tone of voice around them. Some people shout at horses when they don't do what they want. But all that does really is scare them and sometimes makes the horse feel as if they need to defend themselves.

With a horse who is pinning ears or thinking about kicking - can you pause for a moment and figure out what happened to the horse for him to decide he needed to do this? There is always a reason. Maybe they are afraid or frightened. Maybe they have mis-understood something we haven't explained clearly.

We can help a horse to feel comfortable by considering how we approach them. For example, if you want to approach the hindquarters of a horse, start at their head and say hello, then rub down their body until you get to their rump. Don't surprise them by going straight to their hind end and touching them there.

Next time you hear someone saying that a horse is being naughty, or deliberately trying to upset them, try thinking about it in a different way - think to yourself that the horse is just being a horse.

REMEMBER TO SCRATCH & RUB

Think about how your horse likes to be touched as well. Many horses love to be rubbed and scratched. Now maybe not everywhere - but they will appreciate us taking the time to find out their favourite places.

A lot of people slap their horses when they have done well, but this makes no sense to me. Horses get used to it. In fact, their first instinct would be to move away from a slap but they learn that's not being asked of them. I'm sure they would prefer a nice rub on the neck, or scratch on the withers to being slapped hard and loudly.

BE A GREAT TEACHER

Every second you spend with your horse, you are teaching them something. Sometimes it's something good. And sometimes without realising it, you could also be teaching them something not so good! Horses are watching and learning from us all the time. Your bond with your horse will get stronger if you are a kind and fair teacher for them. Get to know your horse so that you understand what things are quite easy for them and what might be a bit more difficult.

Always be patient. If you start to feel frustrated, it can be a good idea to walk away for a break, or do something easier for a little while. Don't ask your horse to do too much at once! And remember to reward the smallest try when they are learning.

If you have learned something new, you like your teacher to say 'well done' and give you a little time to enjoy the moment and feel proud of yourself. It's the same with horses! They love praise.

This might mean stopping work, or releasing your reins, or doing something else. It's about giving them a break. There is an old joke about "eating the elephant":

How do you eat an elephant?? One bite at a time!

If you want to teach your horse something new, or learn something new yourself, it will be easier to understand if you break the task down into small stages.

Let's say you want to teach your horse to put their head down low when you ask. You might start by putting your hand up between their ears and gently putting a little bit of pressure on. As soon as you feel your horse THINK about putting his head down - take your hand away. Give the horse a rub, then try again. In tiny stages your horse will put their head down and after a while they will understand to do it as soon as you ask, without any pressure needed. Just the idea is enough, because they understand what you are thinking.

HORSE BREEDS

There are many horse & pony breeds around the world.

HORSE COLORS

Horses & ponies come in many different colours.

Sorrel Chestnut	Dapple grey	Bay	Blue dun
Grey	Flaxen chestnut	Skewbald	Blue-eyed cream
Black	Dun	Liver chestnut	Red roan
Palomino	Appaloosa	Piebald	Buckskin

How do you make a small fortune in the horse industry? Start with a large fortune

BUYING A HORSE

If you are lucky enough to be able to buy a horse of your own one day, there are some things you can do to find the right new friend. It's exciting to look at all the pictures of pretty horses and ponies for sale but remember that the most important thing is that your new horse has a kind temperament and you will get along with each other.

The heart of your horse is more important than how they look. Colour does not matter! There will be adults who can help you find the right horse. Maybe your riding instructor or someone you know who is very experienced. They will help you to make sure that the horse suits you as a rider and you can handle on the ground. They will look at the horse to make sure they don't seem to have any physical problems.

FINDING AN EXPERIENCED HORSE

- If you are learning to ride, buying an experienced horse is great as they will be able to teach you and take care of you as you learn.
- If you are learning to ride, buying a young and inexperienced horse can often cause issues - a young horse really needs an experienced rider, trainer and teacher to help them learn.

Usually people get a vet to check horses over before buying and that can save a lot of money and worry in the long run.

Here's my number one tip when trying out horses or ponies for sale - always see someone else ride the horse first. I'd go as far as to say that if you can't see someone ride before you get on, just walk away. Better to be safe than sorry! Lots of us who love horses can't afford to buy one. There are other ways to be around them though.

1. You can find someone with a horse who would be willing to share their horse with you, usually for a small contribution and some help with the work.
2. You could get a part-time job at your local riding school.
3. You could work for free at a local stables in return for horse riding lessons.
4. You could get a horse on loan.
5. Go to horse shows or a local centre and watch as much as you can.
6. Study horse books in your local library to increase your knowledge.
7. Offer to muck out stables or clean tack for free for anyone who has a horse
8. Watch horses in a field and observe how they interact with each other

HORSE ANATOMY

A horse's body is very different from ours! Let's take a look at the anatomy of the horse. It's a great idea to learn all the horse's body parts.

Parts of the horse

Labels on the horse diagram: Poll, Crest, Forehead, Withers, Muzzle, Point of hip, Croup, Loin, Back, Chin groove, Dock, Throat latch, Tail, Shoulder, Elbow, Forearm, Stifle, Barrel, Knee, Gaskin, Chestnut, Cannon, Hock, Cannon, Coronet, Fetlock, Ergot, Pastern, Pastern, Hoof, Heel

After a few minutes study, close your eyes & see how many parts of the horse you can remember!

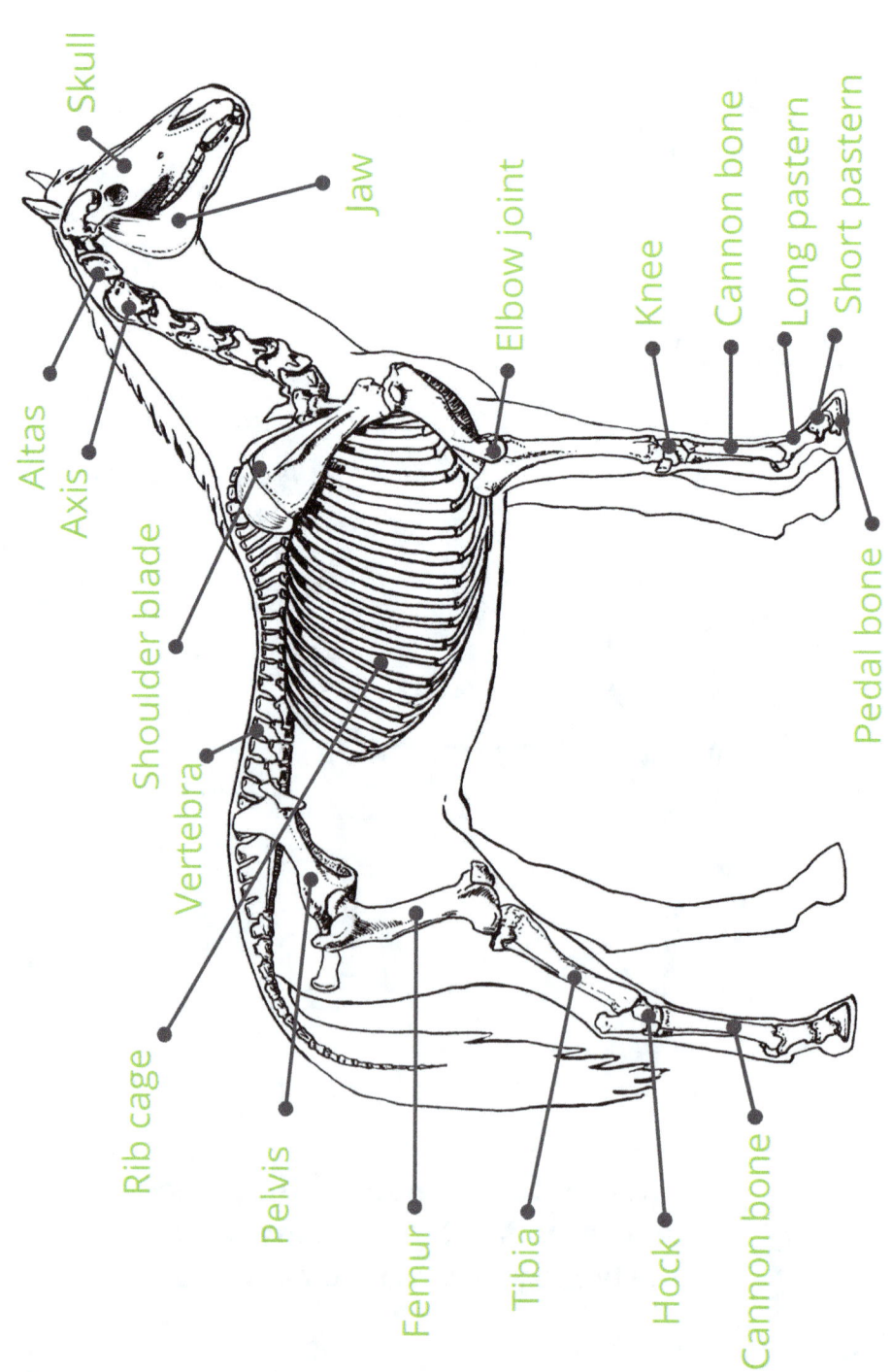

THE EQUINE SKELETON QUIZ

Test your knowledge of the equine skeleton

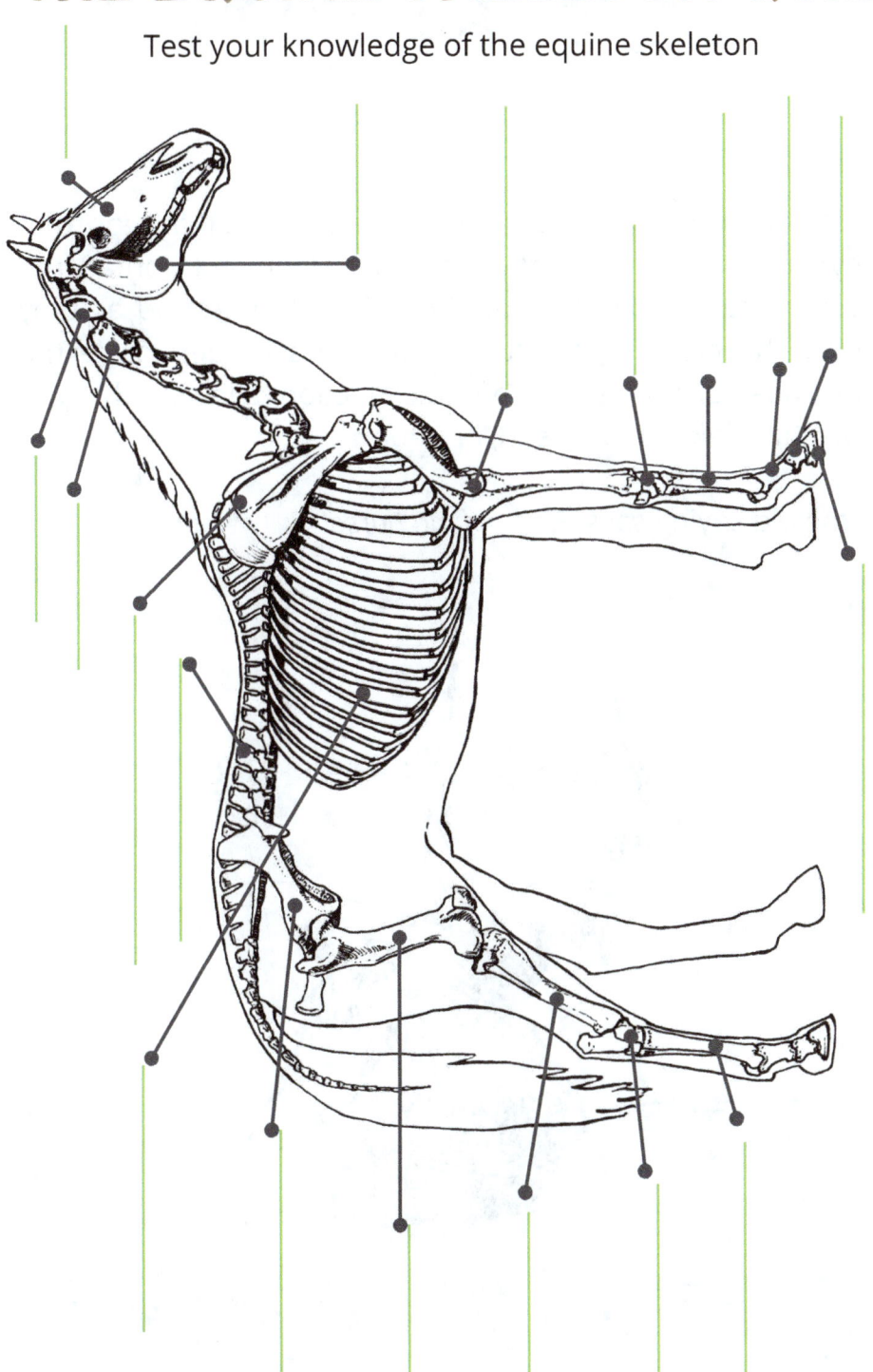

THE HOOF

Your horse's hooves are perfectly designed for the job that they do. They support the horse's weight and spread the pressure caused by the hooves striking the ground as they move. The hooves protect the bone and tissues inside the hoof capsule. They give the horse traction, allowing them to powerfully take off at speed, or jump.

As the old saying says: *No hoof, no horse!*

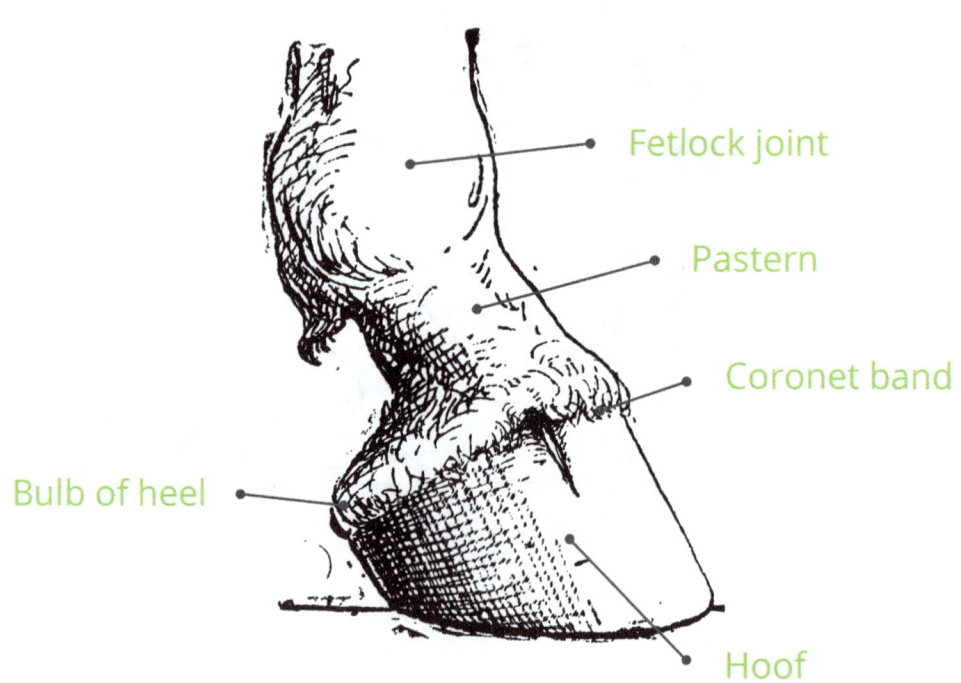

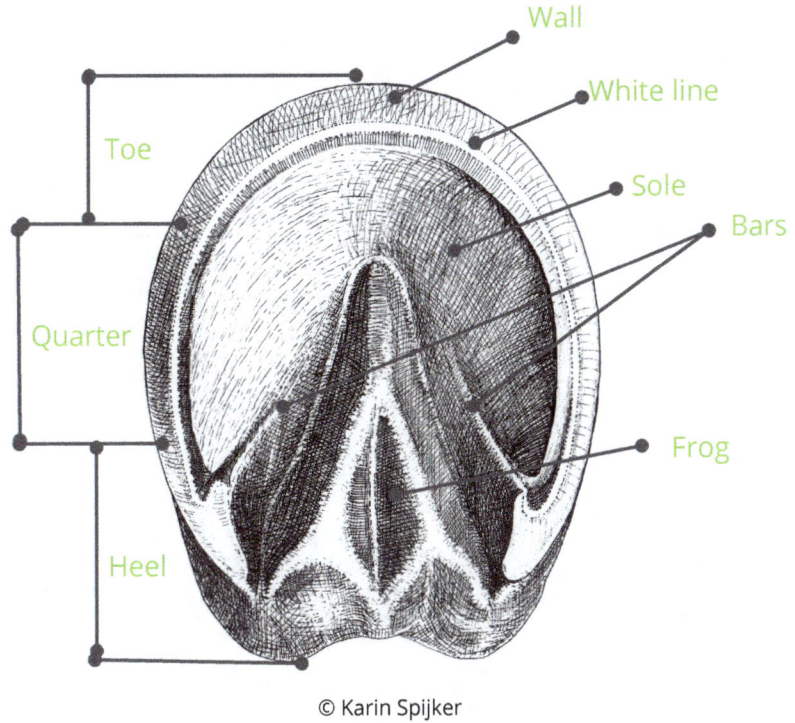

© Karin Spijker

Lift up your horse's hooves daily & pick out any dirt or small stones using a hoofpick. You use a hoofpick going from heel to toe. You do not use a hoofpick going from toe to heel.

YOUR HORSE'S TEETH

- A foal has 12 premolars and 12 incisors = **24 teeth**
- An adult horse has 12 molars, 12 incisors and 12 premolars = **36 teeth**

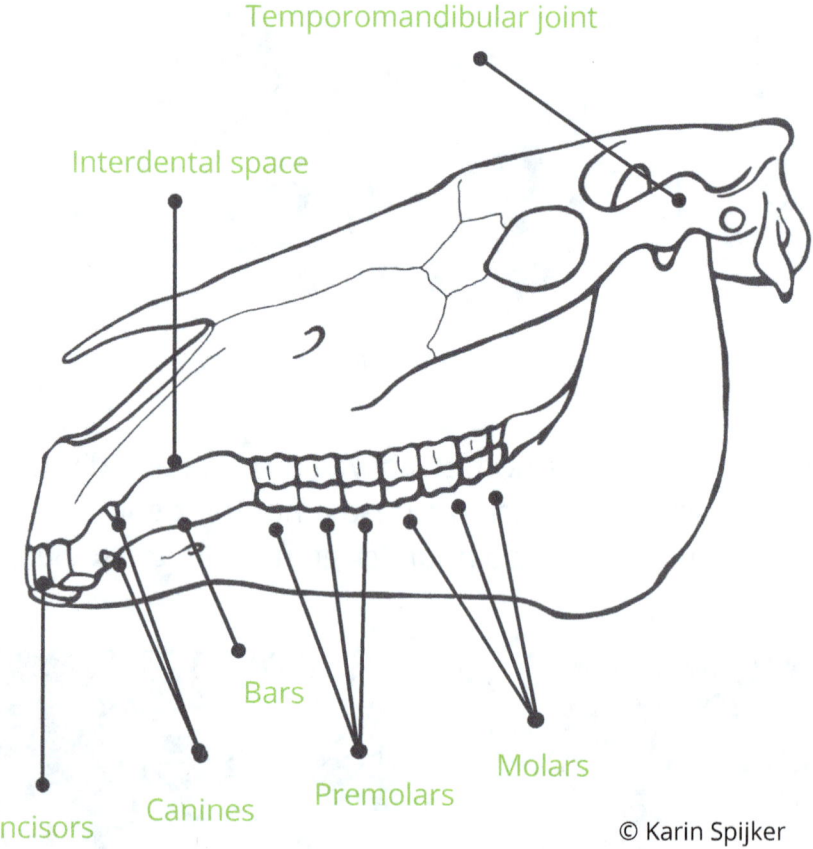

© Karin Spijker

Did you know, we can tell how old a horse is by their teeth! Your vet or equine dentist can do this and should be able to show you how they work out your horse's age from their teeth.

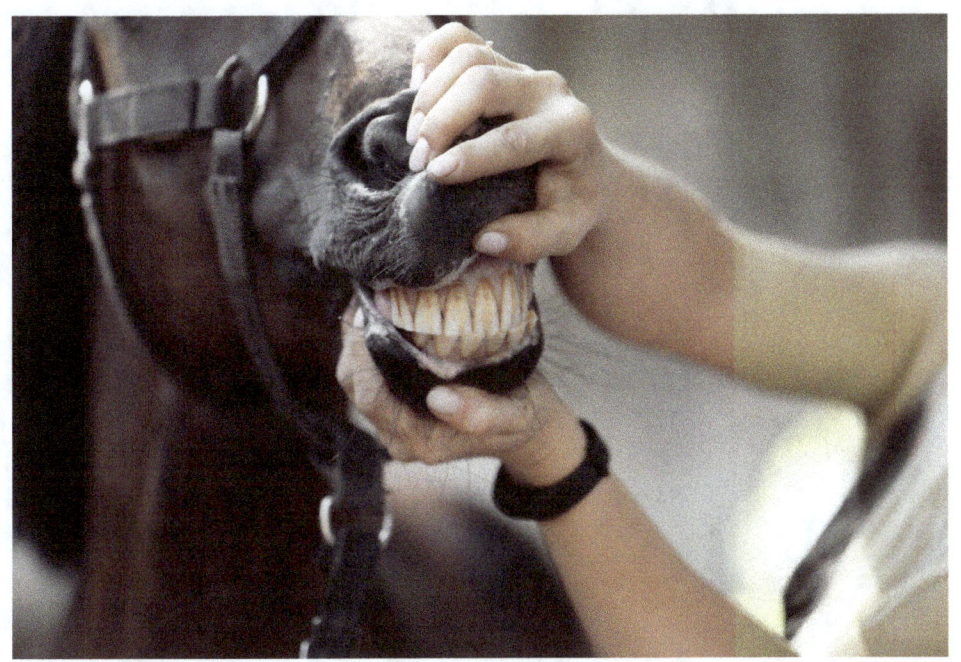

Horses generally have some teeth before they are born. The last of their baby teeth appear by the time they are about 8 months old. Around the time that they reach the age of 2.5 years old their baby teeth start to fall out and are replaced by their adult teeth. By the time they are 5 years old they will have a full set of adult teeth.

Unlike our teeth, horse's teeth keep growing for most of their life. They slow down as they get older and might start falling out. Because the teeth are growing, and constantly being ground down as the horse eats, they can change shape and become sharp or loose. This is why we need to ask an equine dentist or vet to check our horse's teeth at least once a year.

HORSES GROWING UP

When horses are born they are called foals. At that stage in their life they are with their mum and taking milk from her. There comes a time when they leave their mum and then they are called weanlings.

When the horse is a year old they are known as a yearling. This can get confusing because some horses have an "official" birthday on 1st January regardless of when they were actually born! Thoroughbreds are an example of this. A Thoroughbred born in say June still has their official first birthday on the following 1st January and is called a yearling. How strange is that?!

When a horse is 15 years old they start to be known as a veteran. That doesn't mean they are ready to retire though. Some horses keep on working well into their 20's and even 30's!

AT WHAT AGE SHOULD YOU START RIDING A HORSE?

Scientists who have studied physical development in horses have shown us that horses aren't fully grown up until they are 5.5 to 8 years old. **There is no breed that is physically grown up younger than that.** It takes horses' bones and joints years to properly develop.

Because we do not want to hurt our horse's developing body when they are still growing, it is best to wait until your horse is at least 4 or 5 years old to start riding, if we want to give them the best chance of staying healthy into old age.

Some people think it's OK to start riding horses when they are very young, maybe as young as 18 months to 2 or 3 years old, but there is a very high chance you will cause long term damage to your horse's body. I start riding my horses when they are 5 years old.

Let's take a look at when a horse's body is fully developed. It happens at different times for different areas of the body.

This is the minimum development rate for all breeds of horses and ponies. Some horses can still be growing at 7 and 8 years of age. The last thing we want to do is to work a young horse too hard, damage their still growing bones and cause a potential lifetime of injury or pain to the horse.

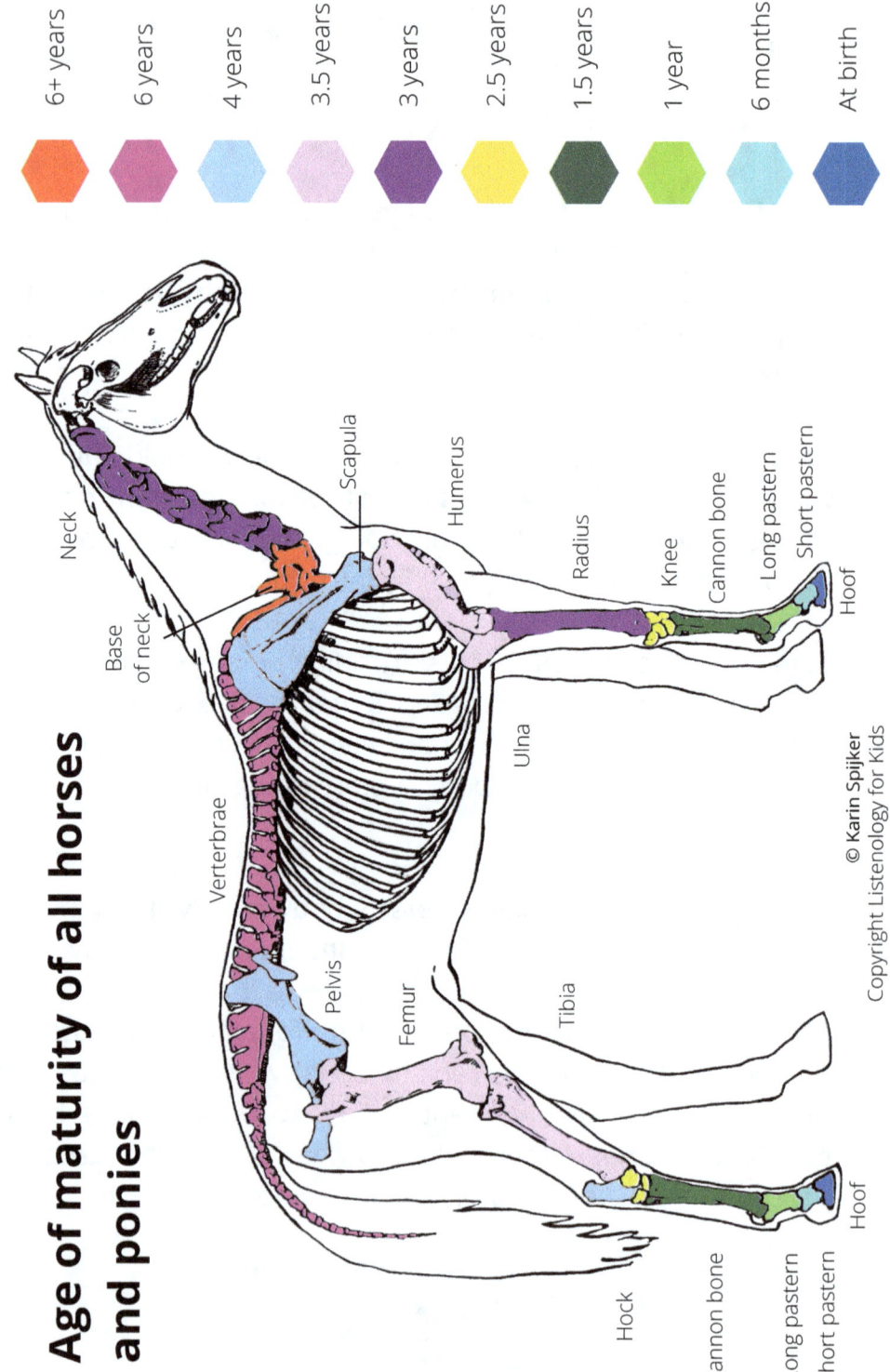

HORSE PEOPLE

Interesting fact: *Did you know that most vets study for 5 years to get qualified?*

If we are lucky enough to own a horse it doesn't matter how much we study, there will still be times when we need help. It's good to be organised, find people that you trust and have their phone numbers handy.

Vet - All horses need to see a vet at some time. If we're lucky it will just be for annual vaccinations to be carried out. Most horses have times when they are sick, or when they get injured in some way, and then we'll need our vet.

Equine dentist - Vets can carry out dental work on horses, but there are also equine dentists who specialise in looking after our horse's teeth. Horses generally need their teeth checked once a year. Younger horses' teeth grow faster, so they will need their teeth checked more often at this stage. The last thing you want is your horse to have a sharp tooth that is pinching his gum, and being really painful! So regular dentist check ups are really important.

Physiotherapist - The physio should check your horse for muscle pain if your horse is exercising hard, or there has been a change in how much work he does. Be sure to ask if there is any back pain, that may indicate there is a saddle fit issue. This needs to be checked on each visit.

Instructor(s) - We probably need an instructor more than our horse does! A good instructor will help you to work with your horse on the ground, or ride, in a way that is best for you and your horse. Even experienced riders can learn from a good instructor. People who don't have horses sometimes ask why have lessons if you've already learned to ride? The truth is we never stop learning how to get better. And no one in the world knows everything there is to know about horses. *We all have to keep learning!*

Have you heard of the Spanish Riding School? Maybe do a bit of research and have a look at information on the Internet. The riders go there when they are 15 - 18 years old and even though they become very advanced horse riders they never stop having lessons.

Saddle fitter - Saddles are there to help the rider to be secure and for them to be comfortable. But - much more important than that - they are there to protect the horse's back and help them to carry us as easily as possible. Horses get sore quickly if their saddle doesn't fit and it can make them start to do things like buck, or refuse to move forward.

Many times when a horse is being called "naughty" for doing things like this, they are actually uncomfortable or in pain. So good horse owners have their horses' saddles fitted properly by a qualified saddle fitter. Horses change shape depending on how fit they are, or whether their weight changes, so saddle fit should be checked regularly, ideally twice a year.

The bit fitter - Bit fitting is a profession that is getting more common and that's a really good thing! Think about how carefully you would want a piece of metal fitted if it was sitting in your mouth. It's the same for horses. A poorly fitting bit can pinch their mouth, damage their teeth and cause ulcers. A well fitting bit will be easy for them to have in their mouth and they will be able to respond better to you when you ride. So it's great now that we can get a well trained bit fitter to visit who will look carefully at a horse's mouth and recommend exactly the best bit for them.

The equine bodyworker - Horses sometimes get aches and pains. They can have busy lives just in the field that we don't always see - running and playing with friends - and sometimes they slip and slide about a bit! They also work hard for us when we ride and work with them. So every now and then they deserve to have someone who really understands how their body works to come and check them over. The bodyworker will give some treatment and often leave the horse's owner with some things they can do themselves. It's worth arranging for them to visit once a year to check your horse over. This is another thing we can do to keep our horses fit and healthy and working happily into old age.

The equine nutritionist - Working out what to feed horses can be a minefield! There are so many different feeds out there and so many people giving us different advice! Luckily we can contact equine nutritionists who are not employed by a particular feed company who can give sound advice. Getting the feed right can help horses with loads of different medical conditions, including the tendency to get laminitis.

The horse book author - The people who write horse books like this can save you a lot of time and effort. We gather up useful information, share our experiences and bring it together in our books. Find horse book authors you like and who talk about caring for horses the way that you want to, and enjoy reading all their books.

The farrier/trimmer - There's a saying, "No hoof, no horse" and it's very true. Horses need to have their hooves in good condition to be able to work properly.

If your horse is shod then they must be cared for by a qualified farrier, and will probably need new shoes around every six weeks. If they are unshod a farrier will also be able to trim their hooves and care for them. With an unshod horse the other option is to use a properly accredited barefoot trimmer (also known as an equine podiatrist). Even unshod horses need regular hoof care, usually on a cycle of 4 - 8 weeks.

How do you decide if your horse needs shoes or not? In the past, putting shoes on all horses was *not* normal. But with more modern times it has become more expected. Shoes are often put on if:

- Your horse's feet wear down very fast (maybe they are on hard surfaces like roads a lot)
- Your horse's feet have a lot of cracks or issues and your farrier said they need shoes to help fix the issues (cracks in horses feet are not good!)
- You are doing very high level competitions and need shoes to improve your performance

However, not all horses need shoes!

- If your horse has healthy feet that have no cracks
- If your horse is rarely lame
- If your horse is not doing a lot of work on roads and their feet are not wearing down unnaturally fast
- If your horse is not doing high level competitions where shoes are required in the rules.
- If your horse needs shoes at certain times of the year, you can also take them off for several months when your horse doesn't need them (no competitions, ec).

Then your horse could be perfectly fine without shoes! All my horses, and many horses I know do great without any metal shoes. Sometimes even if the horse doesn't have good, strong feet, you could also consider to transition them to being barefoot, with proper professional support.

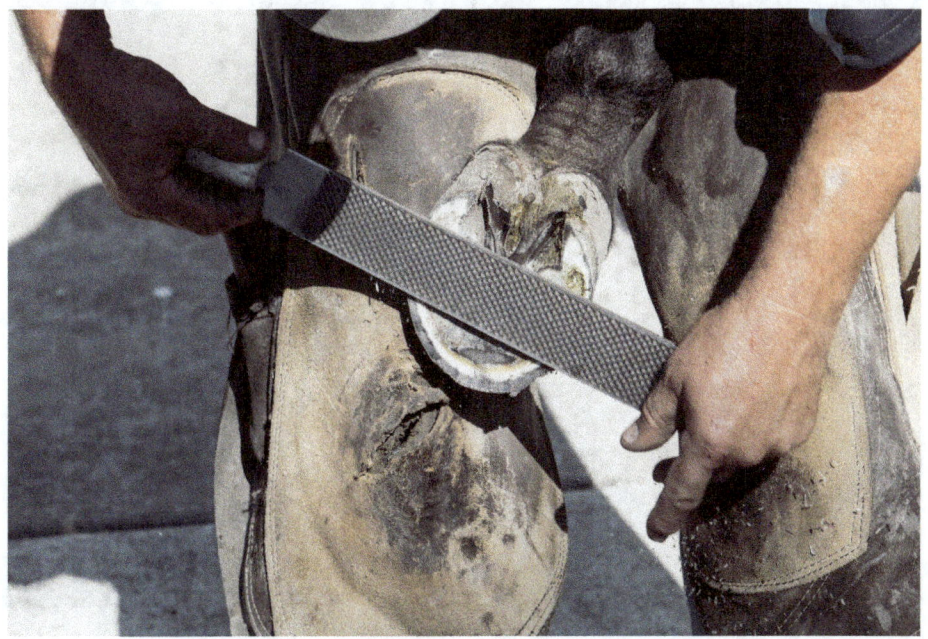

SOMETIMES PEOPLE AREN'T KIND

It's hard to understand, but people aren't always kind to horses and sometimes people aren't always kind to other horse people. Do the best you can for the horses you meet or own, but usually it's best to only offer advice and ideas to other people if you are asked to. Sometimes we can't change all the things, we just change the things we can.

If you are ever in a situation where you see someone being really cruel to a horse, or if someone is unkind or cruel to you - tell an adult you trust and get some help. Don't let anyone make you be unkind to a horse either. If something feels wrong to you it probably is (even if it's been done by an adult or horse professional), so again, if that happens, speak to an adult you trust who can help you.

WHERE HORSES LIVE

Did you know that wild horses can travel 30 - 40 miles in a day while they eat and look for water?

To have a healthy and happy life, where & how your horse lives is very important. Horses need to have space to move around, to be able to gallop and play with their friends. Horses need shelter. This might be natural shelter from trees and hedges, or a man-made shelter.

Some horses come into stables for part of the day or overnight, but it's not good for them to be shut in a stable all of the time. It must feel like being in jail! It would be a little like locking you in your bedroom all day. That would get very boring very quickly. Horses can also start to feel stiff in their joints and get swollen legs if they don't get enough movement in their day. Movement like walking, trotting & cantering around helps to keep your horse healthy.

Horses like the company of other horses and ponies. It's natural for them to groom each other and play. Sometimes they might seem to be arguing a bit. They can be a bit rough with each other by human standards! Male horses tend to play together more than mares do. The boys might rear up and nip at each other's heads and necks. They might even nip at each other's knees and end up kneeling down on the ground.

You can usually tell if a horse isn't playing but is being aggressive to another. They will have their ears pinned back and might be chasing or biting the other horse. The other horse would look distressed. Even though we might have to step in at times like this, remember - they are just horses being horses - they are behaving naturally, it doesn't mean this is a bad horse.

Horses feel safer when they have other horses around them. Watch a group of horses when they sleep in the field. Often some will stay standing on guard while the others lay down to have a sleep. Herd animals feel safer when they are together, they can relax if they know that one of them is looking out for dangers. Physical contact is important to them too. Horses like to groom each other, often by nibbling each other's necks and withers. They will sometimes stand nose to tail to swish flies off each other.

It is very important for all horses to be able to express their normal horse behaviour. To do that they have to have freedom to move about and the company of other horses.

HORSE CARE

It's our job to make sure that the place where our horse lives is looked after properly. If they have a stable it has to be mucked out every day. The horse has to have access to clean water all of the time. Sometimes we have to go out regularly with a wheelbarrow and fork and take all the horse manure out of the field. Horses should be checked at least once a day to make sure they are OK - and twice a day is even better.

If you're thinking of owning a horse - remember that sometimes it is really hard work - especially in winter!

Sometimes you need to get up early to look after your horse, before you go to school. It might be raining and really cold. But your horse needs you, so you have to get used to bad weather. Sometimes when you are tired or hungry, your horse might need extra hay to eat. You have to forget you are tired and hungry, and always look after your horse first.

If your horse is sick but your friends are at a party, you might need to skip the party, and stay at home, making sure your horse is ok. So while having a horse is amazing, there is a lot of work that comes with them. And often we have to do this work when we are tired, wet, cold or hungry - because it's our job to always mind our horses and put them first. No one said owning a horse was easy!

HORSE FOOD

When it comes to eating, horses are very different to us. We need three meals a day and do very well in between times without eating any more. Horses need to have access to forage all day and night, this helps to keep their stomachs healthy. Forage is usually grass, hay or haylage. There are ways to slow down horses who eat too much forage too quickly, but even fat horses need to be able to eat constantly round the clock. Imagine if we tried to eat all day, we'd feel like we were going to explode!

People have come up with lots of different ways to slow down horses eating forage. Here are a few:

- **Hay nets** - a mesh, usually nylon, made into a bag that can be tied up on the wall. Hay nets come with different sized holes, the smaller holes slow down eating even more.
- **Slow hay feeders** - these come in all shapes and sizes. Some are containers with holes that the hay is pulled through or drops out of. Others are containers that have a lid with netting, metal mesh or a plastic moulding that the horses eat through and push down onto the hay.
- **Multiple hay sources** - hay put out at various locations in the field or on a track, so that the horse has to move from one to the other to eat.

When looking at slow feeding methods it's worth having a chat with your equine dentist about your plans. Some of the ideas on the market, for example slow feeders with wire mesh, can be damaging to your horse's teeth.

Horses must have access to clean water at all times. If they are in a stable for any period of time the water in the bucket should be changed every day. Out in the field water troughs and containers must be kept reasonably clean and topped up.

Many horses will have some "hard feed" in a bucket or bowl as well as forage. This will vary depending on where in the world you live. It could include grains, feeds such as bran, and ready mixed feeds. Get some advice on how much hard feed your horse needs. You will usually find this on a bag of mixed feed, vets, feed suppliers and knowledgeable barn/livery yard managers can also help.

Some horses are fed supplements to help with health conditions, such as joint problems or sweet itch. **Usually you would take advice from a professional on feeding supplements, such as the vet or a specialist in the particular ailment.**

Don't overdo the feeds and supplements. Most horses have very simple needs.

If you want to give your horse treats, don't give them by hand. If you do it will encourage and teach your horse to look for food in hands and possibly start to bite. They will enjoy the treats just as much if you put them on the floor or in a bowl to be eaten. Horses aren't designed to eat sweets, so no sugar lumps or mints! Use healthy treats made for horses.

POISONOUS PLANTS

There are many plants that are toxic or seriously poisonous for horses. I can only list a few here, but if you look on the Internet you will be able to find a very long list.

- **Ragwort** - In some countries ragwort is a real problem, covering fields and the verges by roads in yellow when it is flowering. Ragwort is the home of the Cinnabar Moth caterpillar, so we need to have some in the countryside, but it's not good for horses. Ragwort causes liver damage in horses that will build up over time and can make them fatally ill. If there is plenty of other grazing, horses will usually leave ragwort alone. However if it is wilted or dried it loses its taste and then they might eat it without realising what it is.
- **Giant Hogweed** - Giant Hogweed is nasty stuff for humans and horses. If you or your horse touch it you can get a very nasty, painful rash. If eaten it can be fatally toxic. Make sure you have looked at photos so that you can tell the difference between Giant Hogweed and Cow Parsley. Horses love eating Cow Parsley and it won't do them any harm at all.
- **Sycamore seedlings** - Unfortunately sycamore seedlings can be fatally toxic for horses. This is something that has only been understood in fairly recent years and it's a real shame as, certainly in the UK, there are a lot of these beautiful trees about. Sadly, eating sycamore seedlings can be fatal for horses. The seedlings can be mown, pulled up or sprayed (when the horses are not in the field) but it can be hard to control them because the little "helicopters" carry the seeds a long way.

OTHER POISONOUS THINGS TO AVOID

People will feed all sorts of things to horses, thinking they are giving them a treat, and it's amazing what horses deal with. Here is a list of just some of the things I've known to be given to horses that are really bad for them:

- Potatoes
- Onions
- Cabbage
- Broccoli
- Bread
- Chocolate
- Peppers
- Tomatoes
- Lawn clippings

You might be surprised at some of the things that are safe to feed though:

- Bananas
- Cucumber
- Celery
- Oranges
- Watermelon (just the flesh, not the rind)
- Apricots (without the stone)
- Strawberries
- Raisins

If in doubt - check.

A thought - is it really a good idea to give a horse sweets like mints when they contain a huge amount of sugar and horses don't brush their teeth? *Is feeding sugar cubes a good idea?*

Any fruit with a stone in it (like peaches, cherries or avocados) should be avoided because the horse can choke on the stone, or it can cause colic.

Even if it's the good stuff, as a general rule don't feed loads of anything except forage! A couple of apples aren't going to cause harm, but a whole bag might! Carrots are quite high in sugar but a couple won't hurt a horse, a whole sack would not be good though, particularly for laminitics.

HOW TO TELL IF YOUR HORSE IS ILL

Did you know that horses can't physically be sick? If they eat something bad they can't vomit it up to get rid of it.

Life would be so much easier if horses could talk to us, but they can't. So we do our best to understand them when they need us to. If you think that there is something wrong with your horse, speak to an adult as soon as possible to get some help. Here are just a few of the ways that you can tell that your horse is feeling poorly:

Lameness - If your horse isn't walking or trotting evenly on all legs then they are lame for some reason. If the lameness is in a front leg or hoof their head will lift up a bit when that hoof hits the ground. If your horse is lame in a hind leg or hoof they will nod their head when that hoof hits the ground. Sometimes you can pick up lameness when you are riding because your horse won't feel quite right. You will hear their hooves hitting the ground unevenly and you might be able to see their head nodding or throwing lifting. Often the best person to call first is your farrier or hoof trimmer, who will be able to check hooves quite quickly. If the lameness isn't caused by a hoof problem the vet will need to investigate.

There are lameness signs that worry all horse people - signs of laminitis. If a horse is coming down with laminitis they will look lame, often lifting one hoof at a time when standing still. Sometimes they stretch their legs out and rock a bit. At the first sign of laminitis the horse should be taken completely off grass and put in a stable or area with deep soft bedding for them to stand on. They should be fed soaked hay. The vet should be called immediately.

Colic - Many horses will get colic at some time in their lives, it can be extremely serious so we need to be aware of the symptoms. These are the most obvious:

- Pawing at the ground and being restless
- Kicking at the stomach or turning round to nudge at it
- Breathing fast and sweating
- Rolling, or trying to roll
- Stretching out as if about to urinate (wee)
- A high pulse rate (if a thermometer is available an adult might be able to check this).

If a horse is colicking a vet should be called. Wait for their instructions before feeding or trying to treat the colic.

Sore back - Often the first signs we get that our horse has a sore back is when they start to protest when ridden. Some people would say that the horse is playing up if they start to be reluctant to move forward, carry their head high in the air, or to hunch their back or even buck. These things are signs that all is not right with your horse. Maybe their saddle needs re-fitting, maybe they have pulled a muscle playing in the field, but these signs shouldn't be ignored. The saddle fitter or equine bodyworker may be able to help.

Mouth/teeth problems - If your horse starts to be reluctant to be bridled or to put the bit in their mouth. If they start to chew on the bit, open their mouth a lot, push their head down or shake it about when they are being ridden - have a look inside their mouth for sore places or sharp teeth. If you don't feel confident doing that call your equine dentist/vet to check them.

So many people respond to their horse getting fussy in the mouth when ridden by strapping it shut with something like a flash noseband. **I never, ever put anything on my horse's face to keep their mouth shut or still.** There is a reason for what they do *so it would be wrong to hide it.*

If you see your horse dropping chewed hay or feed out of their mouth when they are eating - they also need to have their mouth and teeth checked. This is called "quidding" and is a common sign that the teeth need attention.

Sometimes a horse needs a different bit to be comfortable in their mouth. As mentioned before, when fitting a bit you need to consider the shape of your horse's mouth. If you have access to a bit fitter they are a really great help.

OTHER THINGS TO WATCH OUT FOR

There are other things to watch out for that will tell you your horse isn't feeling quite right:

- Coughing
- Not moving about as much as usual
- Standing on their own a lot with their head down
- Breathing heavily
- Not eating or drinking
- Sweating for no reason

If your horse is sick - tell an adult so that they can call the right person to help - the vet, farrier or dentist maybe.

GROOMING YOUR HORSE

Grooming your horse is a great way to build a bond with them and it's a good chance to check them over and make sure they are OK. Grooming isn't just about making your horse look pretty. You'll also be caring for their hooves, eyes and all of their body.

You can pack an awful lot of brushes, sponges and other tools into a grooming kit! There is much fun to be had buying brushes in your favourite colours! However you can save your pocket money by putting together a basic grooming kit that has just the things that you need to care for your horse. These are the things I have in my grooming kit:

Most horses enjoy being groomed. But if yours doesn't, try to respect that as much as possible. See what you can do to change their mind. Try different brushes for example. Bear in mind that you can't always use the same brush on the parts of their body where they have less fur and will be more sensitive. I have found that a lot of horses who aren't sure about being groomed with brushes respond well to being groomed with my hands. Grooming gloves have rubber palms with "pimples" that are great for this.

Let's have a look at what the items in the grooming kit are for:

Dandy brush - A dandy brush is a heavy duty brush with stiff bristles, which are often nylon. It's great for removing mud and dirt. When you go shopping have a look at what is on offer, there are some modern brushes that do the same job as a traditional dandy brush, made completely of plastic, that are very efficient.

Hoof pick - Horses' hooves should be picked out daily. Sometimes this isn't possible because of how and where your horse lives, but do it as often as you can. Use the hoof pick to remove mud, stones and other things that have got caked up on the sole and around the frogs. Make sure that you use the pick starting from the frog and down towards the toe, never scrape towards the frog in case your hand slips and you cause damage. If you see anything about the hoof that worries you get some advice from the farrier or a knowledgeable adult. If you smell a really horrible smell your horse probably has a touch of thrush, which can cause problems if left for a long time, but can be treated.

The really important thing about picking out hooves is that your horse has to be good about picking up their legs and holding them up while you work on their hoof. If your horse isn't good about this, especially if they try to kick out, ask for some help. My advice is that children and young people should always wear a protective helmet when handling horses, just in case.

Metal curry comb - The metal curry comb does two jobs. You can use it for removing caked on mud from your horse. Be gentle when you do this and don't use it on the bony parts of the legs, or on the face. It just loosens up the mud enough so that you can use a brush to finish the job.

The other thing a metal curry comb can be used for is cleaning your brushes while you are grooming. I was always taught to brush my horse 3 times with the brush, then swipe the brush over the curry comb to clean off the dirt and hairs.

There are several different types of curry comb to choose from. When you are choosing, look at the design and decide which you think will feel best to your horse.

Body brush - Body brushes have softer and shorter bristles than a dandy brush. They lift scurf and loose hairs up and distribute oils across the horse's coat to make it shine. During the winter the body brush should only be used on horses that get stables and/or rugged regularly. Horses that live out, either without rugs or only wearing rugs occasionally, should not be brushed with a body brush because it will reduce their natural protection. In the summer, everyone can be made shiny with a body brush!

Mane and tail brush - Mane and tail brushes usually look quite similar to human hair brushes and a lot of horse people actually use human hair brushes on their horses! The bristles are flexible and widely spaced. It's lovely to keep your horse's mane and tail looking lovely, just bear in mind that too much pulling and tugging a brush through it can break the hairs and pull them out. So if you want a long mane... don't attack it too hard! When you are grooming your horse's tail, stand to the side of their rump and hold the tail to the side, rather than standing directly behind them.

A rubber curry comb or grooming gloves with pimple palms - These will do a similar job to a metal curry comb, but they aren't much use for cleaning brushes. They are both great for removing dry mud. The other great thing they do is to help you to give your horse a lovely massage. Just try and see which parts of their body they like rubbed with these tools. It's a lovely way to spend relaxed time together.

Sponges - At least two sponges that you will wash to keep clean after every use. One is for your horse's face - nose, eyes, around the mouth if needed. The other is for the other end of their body... their dock and private parts. You can buy packets of wipes for these jobs, but that's not very kind to the environment.

Mane and tail detangler - A good detangler will make your life so much easier, especially in the winter when your horse gets windswept, rubs their mane in the mud and generally enjoys being messy. It's not strictly a basic essential, but very handy all the same. Make sure your horse is good with sprays before spraying the detangler on their mane and tail. Then work it in with your fingers before brushing. If your horse is afraid of sprays, that's something to work on. Meanwhile you can spray the detangler on your brush or your hands, and then put it on the mane and tail.

Fun homework: Horses have favourite brushes. Next time you groom a horse try different brushes and watch their reaction to see which they like best.

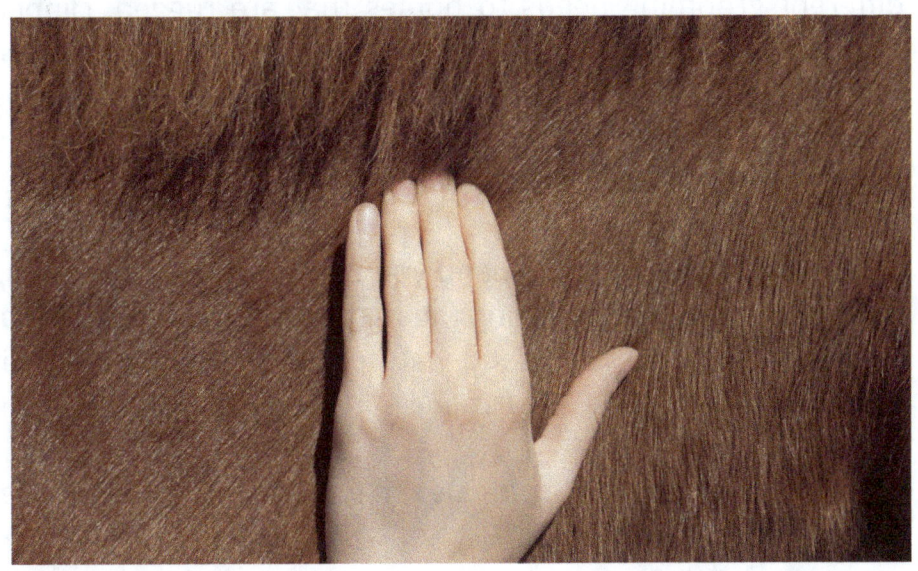

Remember the most important tool of all: your hands!

Feel for lumps, bumps and scrapes with your fingers as you groom. You may not always see everything under all that hair, but your fingers will feel if there are clumps of mud or maybe a scab or cut.

HORSE RUGS

Horses that live out and often don't wear rugs will have different grooming needs to horses that are rugged, clipped and spend time in the stable. Be particularly aware of this in the winter, when horses that live out without rugs will need the natural oils in their fur to help keep them warm and dry. So do not groom them too much.

If your horse is not clipped, and you decide to put a heavy rug on them, you will be reducing the natural oils in their coat that help to keep them warm and waterproof and flattening their fur. *So maybe that's not the best idea.*

Just because we feel cold, doesn't mean our horses feel cold!

If your horse is warm enough and doesn't need a rug, you do not need to put on a rug as they can overheat. Over-heating a horse is considered by some experts to be worse than them getting a bit cold. Horses that are over-rugged can look quite fed up and stand around not doing much. They can sweat under the rug, which is uncomfortable for them and can cause skin problems.

SADDLES & BRIDLES

Interesting fact: *The Guiness Book of Records records that the highest price ever paid for a saddle is $653,234 (about £432,300). It was sold at an auction for a charity and belonged to the Crown Prince of Dubai, Hamdan bin Mohammed Al Maktoum.*

Saddles and bridles are part of your horse's "tack". You will see horses wearing all sorts of saddles, bridles and other equipment. But to get started things don't have to be complicated. You need a saddle and bridle to ride your horse.

First of all, remember that the tack your horse wears needs to fit them well and be comfortable. You do not want any pinching or rubbing. It also has to be right for you. This is where a good saddle fitter comes in. They will visit to look at your horse and you to decide on what will work for you, then see you riding in the saddle to check that all is well.

Bridles need to fit properly too.

Your horse's head is very sensitive and an uncomfortable bridle will make it hard for them to respond well when ridden.

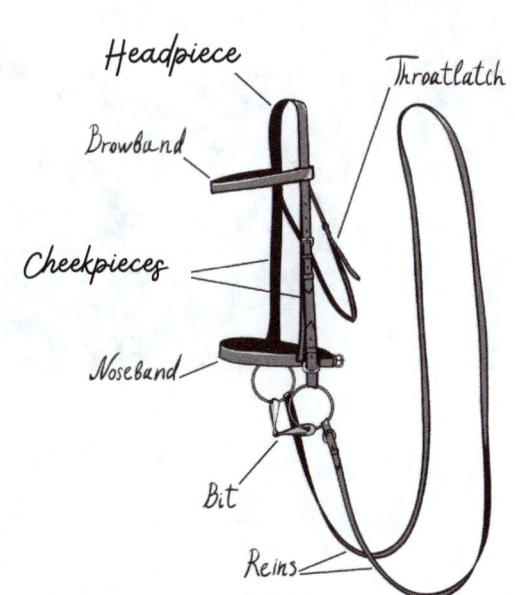

HOW TO FIT A BRIDLE

You might want to leave your horse's halter or headcollar on and tie them up when first fitting a bridle, or have someone hold them for you. Horses are great at wandering off at the wrong moment! Bear in mind that sometimes you need to mix and match with bridles, not all cob size bridles fit all cobs. Some horses need different parts of the bridle in different sizes. My friend's Arab horse wears a pony bridle with a full size browband!

THE CHEEK PIECES AND BIT HEIGHT

Put the bridle on your horse's head. A lot of people will tell you that you should adjust the cheek pieces so that the bit makes 2 or even 3 wrinkles in the corner of the horse's mouth. If you have had a visit from a bit fitter they will have advised on how your horse's bit should sit. However, if you put the bit in and lift your horse's lips to see for yourself you will be able to judge whether it is sitting well in the gap between your horse's teeth. That shows you how long the cheek pieces need to be, regardless of how many wrinkles appear in the lips. However, if you see 3 wrinkles or even more you might want to look again, it's unlikely that will be right.

THE BROWBAND

The browband should be sitting about ½" to 1" below the front of the horse's ears. It should be long enough so that it rests lightly on the horse's head, not tight. Also though it shouldn't stick out and move about when the horse moves.

THE NOSEBAND

The position of nosebands varies a bit depending on which noseband you are using. A lot of people don't use any noseband at all. A cavesson noseband is pretty standard and it should sit at a point about ½" to 1" below the horse's cheekbone. A noseband should never be too tight - you should be able to put one finger in between the noseband and the horse's jaw (two fingers if you have small fingers). The noseband shouldn't interfere with the horse's breathing, or the action of the bit.

There are a lot of nosebands available that sit in front of the bit. Some are marketed as helping the horse keep the bit in place, others as a way of keeping a horse's mouth shut if they tend to open it. The question is - if a horse can't hold a bit comfortably in its mouth, or if a horse keeps opening its mouth - why do they feel the need to do that? Maybe the answer doesn't lie in holding their mouth closed, but in getting a bit fitter out to find the best bit for them? I think that strapping mouths closed causes horses to be tense and is never needed. **Horses should be able to open their mouths. They should be able to yawn and they should be able to open their mouth to show us if they are uncomfortable.**

Things like this can be hard to deal with when you are young, and you aren't always in control of what happens with the horses around you, even with your own. We can all only do what we can, do our best for the horse. If we can't change one thing then there will be other ways we can do little things to make their lives as easy and comfortable as possible.

THE THROATLATCH

Buckle up the throatlatch so that you can fit 4 fingers between it and the horse's jaw. Don't have the throatlatch looser than this because it has an important job to do - it is designed to keep the bridle on the horse's head if need be, for example if the rider falls off. It mustn't be too tight or it would interfere with the horse's breathing.

THE BIT

There is no "one size fits all" with bits. The bit you need will depend on the shape of your horse's mouth, the job they will be doing and how you ride. Before deciding on what bit to use look inside your horse's mouth.

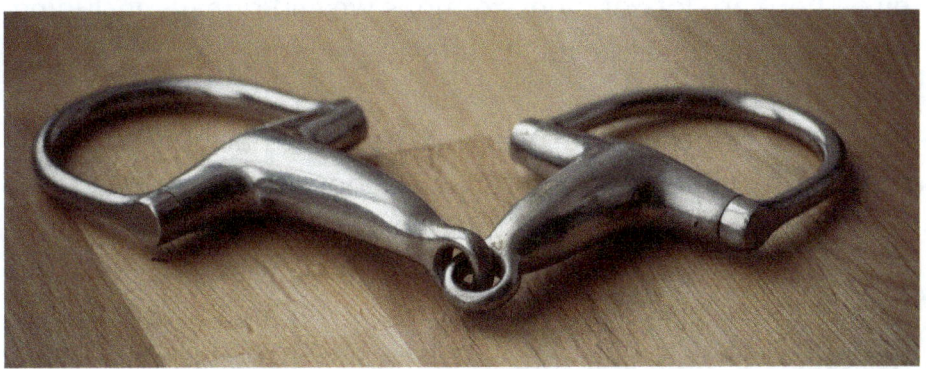

- Look at your horse's tongue - is it quite small and thin, or is it big and fat, taking up most of the space in their mouth? Is there actually room for a bit in there as well? Ask your dentist for advice here too.
- Feel the bars with your fingers, they can feel quite sharp, in which case any bit may be uncomfortable for them.
- The wrong bit can cause damage. It can make teeth sharp, cause ulcers and bruise the horse's mouth.
- Also think about the action of the bit, you can ask someone to put the bit on your arm and move it as it would when riding. It might come as a surprise, but a single jointed snaffle will pinch your arm. How does that feel on the horse's tongue?

A visit from a professional bit fitter can be a great investment in your horse.

RIDING WITHOUT A BIT

Riding without a bit in your horse's mouth may be an option. To be safe you and your horse need to be properly trained to do this, but many horse people around the world never use bits. There are lots of bitless options we can ride in - including western-style bosals, rope halters and sidepulls.

Before you ride without a bit make sure that you have the basics firmly in place for safety. Your horse should bend their neck softly without twisting their head or neck. You should be able to bend them and disengage their hind end easily. They should turn easily and halt or come down a gait without any hesitation or pushing into your hands. If your horse feels heavy in your hands you probably need to do more work before venturing out of the arena.

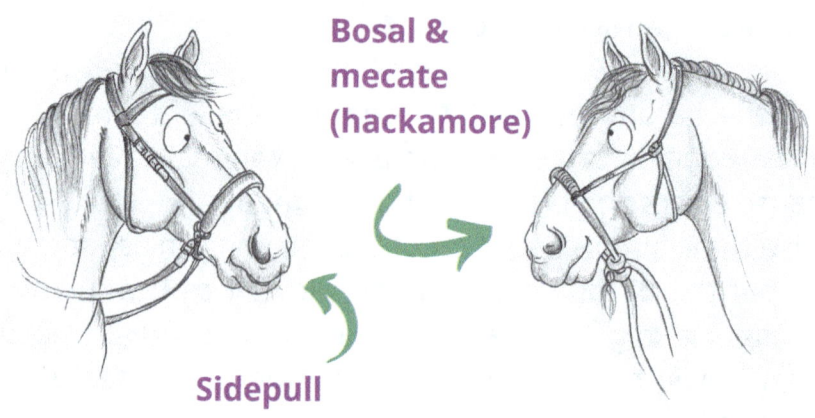

Bosal & mecate (hackamore)

Sidepull

RIDING WITH A ROPE HALTER

A correctly fitted rope halter.

Rope halters are often the first thing that people use when starting to ride without a bit. They are pretty simple, a knotted halter that can be used for ridden work. The lead rope is knotted to make reins, or some use clip-on reins.

Design - There are various designs of rope halter. I think the most simple is probably the best. This would have no extra knots on the nose. It would possibly have a braided noseband so that it sits more softly on the nose. The rope would not be hard and harsh, but nice and flexible.

Fit - Rope halters must be well fitted. The throat piece should sit behind the horse's cheek, rather than on it. The noseband should sit above the end of the fragile nasal bone and fit as closely as it can with the horse able to comfortably open their mouth. **I recommend that you use a rope that does not have a clip, so that it doesn't swing about.**

What to avoid - Rope halters don't break - there is a reason why cowboys carry knives on their belts! So if you are riding in a rope halter be aware of where your ropes and reins are at all times. Do not let your horse graze with the rope reins over their head in case they put their leg through. Keep hold of your reins while riding and don't let your horse drag along with their head at their knees. If you stop, be careful about where and how you tie up your horse. If you travel <u>do not</u> tie up your horse in the trailer or lorry in a rope halter.

RIDING WITH A HACKAMORE (BOSAL & MECATE)

A good hackamore (or jaquima) is a powerful tool that can be used very sensitively for refined riding, and can be a bit of a disaster in the wrong hands! If you can get some expert help getting started riding in a hackamore it's well worth doing. If not, look at videos from experts like Jeff Sanders or Stephen Halfpenny.

Design - I only recommend one style of hackamore, which is the style used in the California Vaquero tradition. They will be expensive to buy but properly cared for will last a lifetime. You should buy from a reputable seller who will advise on fitting. The bosal will be soft (but not floppy!) and flexible so that you can shape it for your horse. There will be many plaits, making it soft on the horse's nose. The mecate (used to form the reins and leadrope) can be made of different materials including horse hair, alpaca wool and paracord.

Fit - You will learn how to shape your hackamore so that it fits your horse's head snugly but comfortably. It will fit in a similar way to a hat on your head. This will be kind to your horse and make your signals through the reins clear. The hanger over the ears may need some adapting with an extra strap to keep it away from the eyes, and sometimes riders add another rope or strap to hold the bosal steady when leading from it.

What to avoid - The big thing to avoid is badly made bosals - which can be both cheap or very expensive! They will be useless to you and a waste of money. They aren't comfortable for the horse and they won't help you with refined riding. Also when you are riding be aware that you should avoid riding with a feeling of constant contact in your hands. When riding in a bosal the "neutral" position is not like an "English" contact, it should just be the weight of the reins.

RIDING WITH A SIDEPULL

After the rope halter, the sidepull is probably the most simple version of a bitless bridle. They often look like a conventional bridle that just happens to not have a bit. They can be made from different materials including leather, rope and nylon.

Design - Sidepull designs are all pretty much the same. The main headpiece is shaped in much the same way as a bridle or rope halter. They usually have a browband. The reins are fixed on the side of the noseband so that they give direct "sideways" signals. Sometimes they have an attachment for a second set of reins, giving a slight curb action.

Fit - The fit of a sidepull is the same as the fit of a conventional bridle. The browband should be wide enough to be comfortable and to avoid pinching the ears.

What to avoid - Avoid designs where the noseband is big and baggy because they will move too much and your signals won't be clear. Make sure that the noseband is not too low, it should sit on the nose above the fragile nasal bone. Also avoid riding with a constant pressure, try to make the neutral place just the weight of your reins.

HOW TO FIT A SADDLE

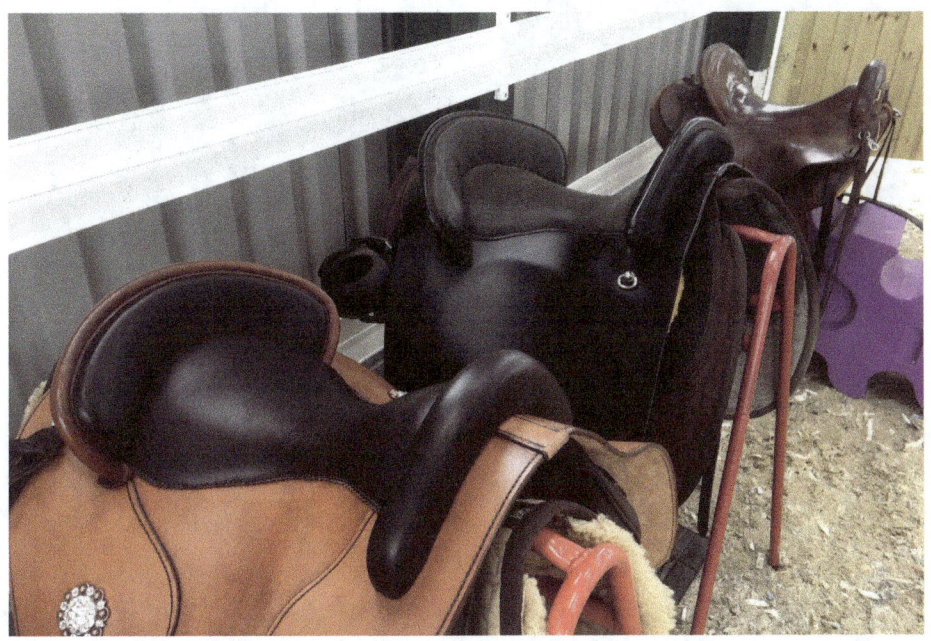

Saddles come in many different shapes and styles. There are western saddles, dressage saddles, saddles with trees, saddles without trees, saddles for general purpose riding, saddles for endurance riding - the list is endless!

Saddles with trees are saddles that have a rigid structure under the leather and padding that is shaped to fit as well as possible to your horse's back. Treeless saddles do not have this rigid part, and are used with special pads underneath to protect your horse's back.

The most important thing when you're buying a saddle is to get it properly fitted by a trained and reliable saddle fitter. There are some things you can check for yourself:

- Make sure that the saddle fits you. It shouldn't be too large so that you slide around, or too small so that you can't move at all!
- The saddle should be comfortable for you. Your legs and knees shouldn't feel sore or twisted and your legs shouldn't get pinched anywhere.
- The saddle has to fit your horse well and they should be able to move freely forward when you ride in it.
- It shouldn't be too wide so it doesn't protect your horse's spine, or too narrow so that it pinches your horse's back, shoulders or withers.
- When you are riding the saddle should stay in place and not bounce or move about.

There are lots of different types of saddles: English (dressage, jumping or general purpose), western, racing, treeless, endurance, stock and many more. The most important thing is that the saddle is comfortable for you and your horse, and is suitable for what you and your horse want to do.

Parts of the saddle

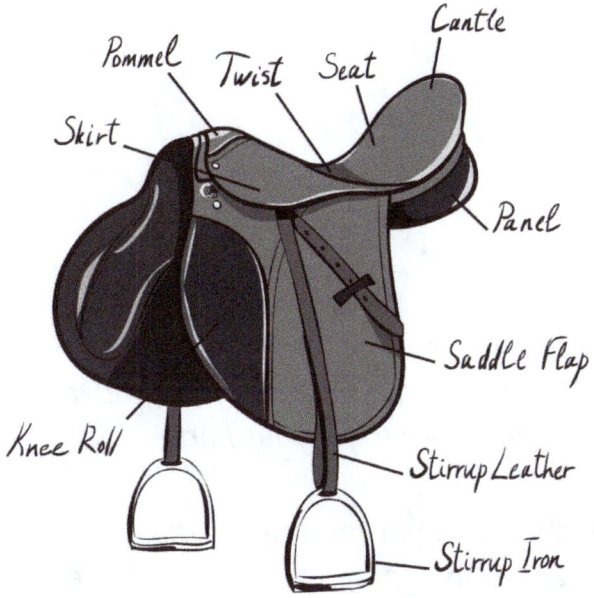

Parts of the western saddle

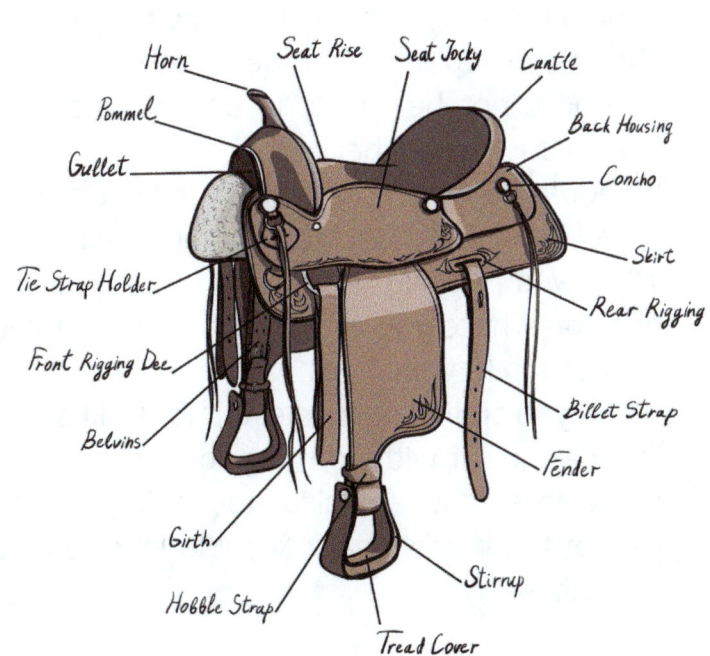

YOUR PERFECT SADDLE...

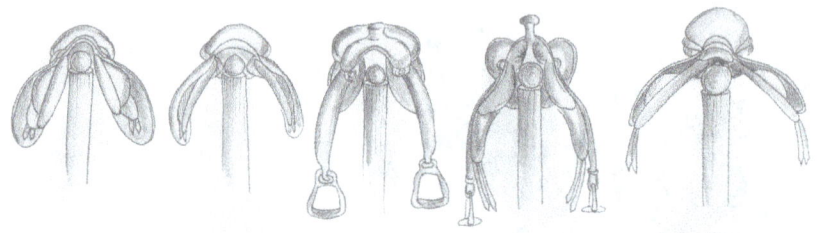

Horses and saddles come in lots of different sizes, from very narrow to super wide! This can make it tricky to find a saddle that is exactly the correct width for your horse.

- Your perfect saddle should fit your horse.
- Should fit your weight & height and you should feel comfortable and confident when riding. The saddle should not be too big or small for you.
- Your legs and knees should not get sore when you ride.
- Should not slip left or right on the horse.
- Should not slip up the horse's neck or backwards.
- It should not be too long on your horse's back (can make your horse's back sore)
- It should be the correct width for your horse - not too narrow and not too wide (both are bad!).
- When you ride the saddle should naturally put you in a position where you can draw a line from your shoulder to your hip to your heel.
- When you sit in the saddle, if it looks like you are sitting in an armchair with your legs out the front, you are out of balance. You are also not sitting on the strongest part of the horse's back & could lead to back injury for your horse.

AVOID GADGETS & SHORTCUTS

There are some other kinds of tack people use sometimes, called gadgets. **Gadgets force your horse to move in a certain way and are not good for your horse's muscles and may even cause pain.** Sometimes people *(even experienced people)* try to use gadgets to force a horse to round his body or tuck his nose in to his chest, or carry his head lower to the ground. This is very bad for your horse's health and should be avoided at all costs. There are no short cuts to good horsemanship.

DAILY SADDLE CHECK

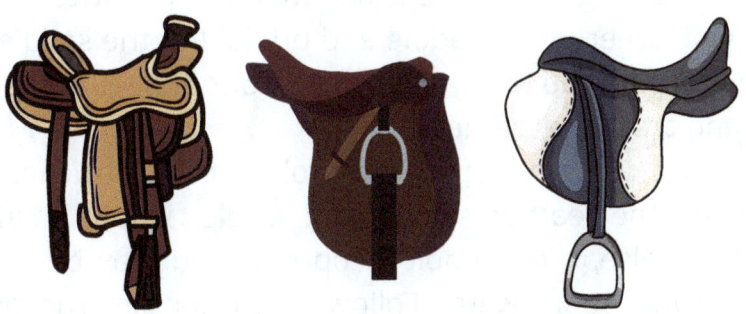

Horses bodies change in shape over time. Saddles can also develop wear & tear. Every day before you put your saddle on your horse and after your ride, you should run your hand gently over your horses back where the saddles would lie, and look for any spots that are sore.

TAKING CARE OF YOUR TACK

Look after your tack well and it will keep you safe and comfortable for many years. Every time you ride at least wipe off sweat and mud and wash the bit. To give your tack a full clean you just need a sponge, a soft cloth, leather conditioner, some water and saddle soap.

- Take the bridle apart, remove the girth and stirrup leathers from the saddle.
- Wet the sponge, squeeze it out well and use it to sponge off the leather in the saddle and bridle. Put the saddle and bridle to one side to dry, but not in front of heat as that can dry and crack the leather.
- If you are using a leather girth follow the instructions for cleaning the leather saddle and bridle. If it is made of anything else, for example neoprene, you may be able to clean it with soapy water. Follow the maker's instructions.
- Wash the stirrups and bit.
- When the saddle and bridle leather parts are dry put the saddle the saddle soap on with the soft cloth. Only put on a small amount at a time and gently rub it on moving the cloth in circles (where possible).
- When you've covered all of the leather, use a clean bit of the cloth to wipe off any saddle soap that hasn't vanished.
- Apply the leather conditioner according to the instructions on the bottle or pot.

When you are cleaning tack, or tacking up your horse, make sure you watch out for any damage or stitching coming apart. It's important to keep your tack in good repair to keep you and your horse safe.

Top tip - when you are tacking up your horse, be gentle and take your time. Don't do the girth/cinch up too tightly at first.

Either take your horse for a short walk around or pull their front legs forward one at a time to make sure your horse is comfortable and not being pinched. Then you can gently finish tightening the girth/cinch.

If you are riding at a riding school see if you can groom your horse and learn how to put their tack on. They are very important skills to learn.

HORSE SAFETY

First of all, a word about staying safe around horses. The first rule is - if you are ever in a situation where you are not sure if you will be safe - stop! Go and find an adult who can help you.

Second let's talk about what to wear:

Sensible, sturdy footwear - for horse care you might wear wellies, but for riding you need to wear riding boots, or a strong shoe with enough heel to stop your foot going through the stirrup. Never wear sandals, flip flops or trainers when handling horses. They don't give you enough protection. You can get boots with protective toe caps, which aren't a bad idea.

Gloves - gloves might not be considered essential, but my advice is to consider wearing them, particularly when you are leading horses about. If your horse gets worried and runs away from you this might save you getting rope burns! Sometimes it is recommended that we wear gloves for riding, and some riding schools will insist on it. Hopefully your horse won't be pulling on the reins enough to hurt your hands, if they do maybe get some lessons with a good trainer.

A protective helmet/riding hat - a lot of riding schools and barns/livery yards have a rule that children and young people should wear a protective helmet at all times when handling or riding horses. I would agree that is a sensible thing to do.

High visibility clothing - if you are going to ride out, even if you aren't going on roads, high viz clothing is a really good idea. It will help road users to see you more easily. If you're unlucky and part company with your horse when you are out in the countryside it will make you easier to see if you need rescuing. You can get tabards, jackets, exercise rugs and bands for your horse as well. The more high viz you wear the easier you will be seen. Be seen, be safe!

GROUNDWORK

Groundwork is a really good way to build the relationship between you and your horse. It also helps to keep your horse fit and supple. Groundwork prepares you and your horse to be safe whether you are on the ground or riding. I think every horse and horse person should do groundwork!

TOP 3 SAFETY TIPS

- Wear a hard riding hat when doing groundwork.
- Be able to lead your horse from both sides (left and right).
- Never wrap your lead rope around your hand. Instead, fold the rope so the rope can never tighten around your hand.

SAFETY ON THE GROUND

When you are with your horse on the ground keep these things in mind to keep you safe:

- Your horse needs to be able to see you. Make sure they know where you are by touching and talking to them. When you pick out their hooves don't crouch right down near the ground, stay standing and just bend from the waist.
- Learn where your horse's blind spots are. They see differently to us because their eyes are on the side of their head. This means that they have blind spots directly in front of them, directly behind them and underneath their head and neck.
- Of course, horses can't see what we are doing under their bellies either! So when grooming your horse's tummy run your hand down their side to touch their belly before you start brushing. Don't duck your head right under their tummy either, it's not a good place to be!
- When you are coming up behind your horse, talk to them so that they know you are there, because as we know they might not be able to see them. It's better to approach from the side if you can.
- Hug your horse from the side rather than standing in front of them, under their head.
- Remember to speak kindly and calmly around your horse. Don't shout, scream or make loud noises. Walk, don't run. It's not fair to startle them when they should be relaxed with you.
- Whenever you are around more than one horse, be aware of where they are. Don't stand between two or more horses - if one decides to move the other you might get squashed!

MAKE THE BEST OF YOUR TIME ON THE GROUND

1. Get into the habit of **checking your horse over every day for cuts or lumps and bumps.** It doesn't take long and is really worth doing.
2. When you approach any horse say "hello" politely first - to do that **put your hand out towards them palm down and let them approach and sniff you.**
3. When you are leading your horse, **think about how soft you would like the reins to feel when you are riding and work for that same soft feel in your lead rope.** Walk shoulder to shoulder with your horse, with a bit of a "smile" in the lead rope. You shouldn't need to hold tight or take hold of the lead rope under your horse's chin. Praise your horse for walking nicely with you.
4. **If you are approaching something that seems to be worrying your horse, put yourself beside your horse, between them and the scary thing.** It will help them to feel confident and also be safer for you if they decide they need to jump away from the thing that has them bothered.

Walk your horse in safe places where you can relax together. It's fun to take your horse for walks, they like going on a bit of an adventure and the more you do this the more confident they will become. It might also help your confidence.

I say that horses have "comfort" zones that affect how they feel and behave. Knowing about this will help you to understand how to help your horse if they get worried, when you are walking with them on the ground, or riding.

- When they are in the Comfort Zone they are in a place where they feel relaxed and happy and will walk along wherever you want to go. Usually this will be around the barn, stables and fields where their friends are. More experienced horses can be comfortable and relaxed much further away from home, they have a big Comfort Zone.
- If you feel your horse start to get a bit anxious - their head goes up, their breathing gets a little bit faster, they aren't taking as much notice of you as they were - you are entering the Not So Sure Zone. This is where you need to listen to your horse and be ready to help them.
- The third zone is the Danger Zone. This is where the horse gets really worried and can't concentrate on what their human wants at all. They don't feel safe and it makes them scared. This is a place you should try to avoid being because, as you might know, when horses get scared they get hard to handle. They might push you over, spook or even run away.

When you are aware of the 3 Comfort Zones you can learn how to deal with them. Spend most of the time you are with your horse working in their Comfort Zone. If there are places where they get a bit worried and go into the Not So Sure Zone, spend a little bit of time working with them there, but only do what feels safe. Then take them back into a place where they are in their Comfort Zone. Stay away from the Danger Zone. If you find yourself there go back to somewhere your horse feels safe and you can handle them safely. Ask for help from an adult if you need to.

It's really important to know that it's OK to ask for help! Any time you feel uncomfortable, unsure or unsafe - get some help.

FUN ACTIVITIES YOU CAN DO ON THE GROUND

Polework exercises are brilliant for developing groundwork. The work you do on the ground will help you when you are in the saddle. While you are doing polework think about how little it can take for your horse to do the exercises. On the ground if you can, work with about a metre, or even 2 metres, of rope between yourself and the horse. Take your time and let your horse have a nice rest and think when you've done an exercise.

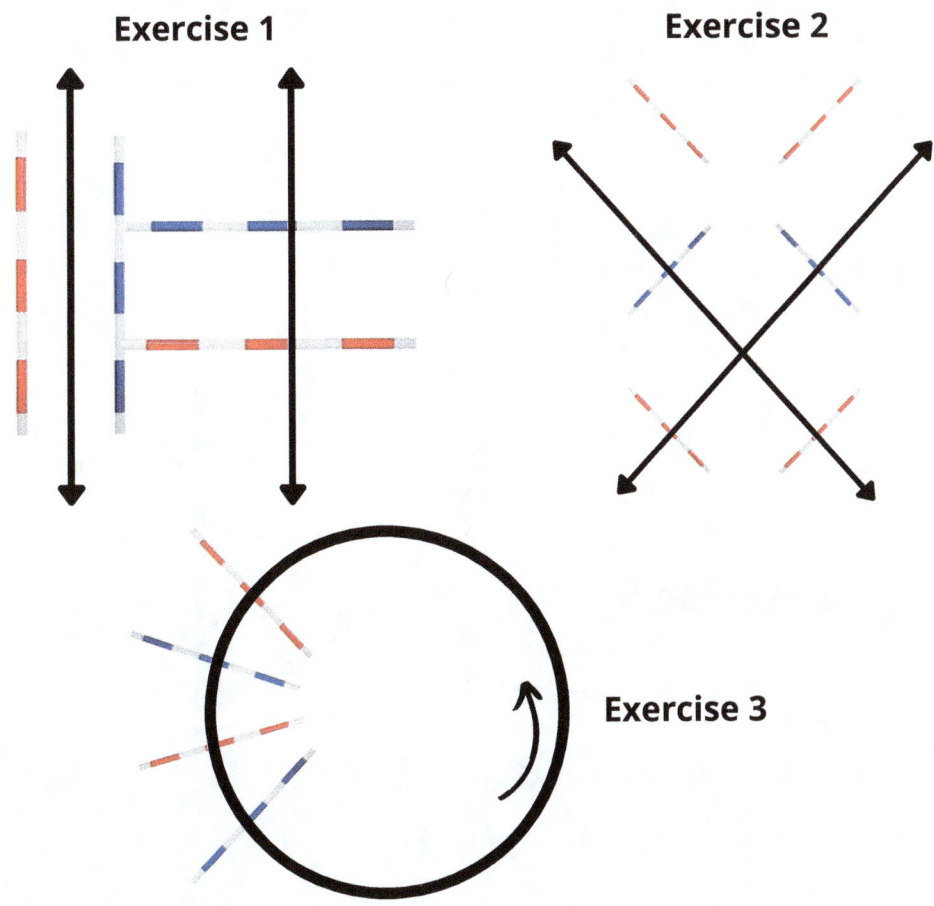

Exercise 4

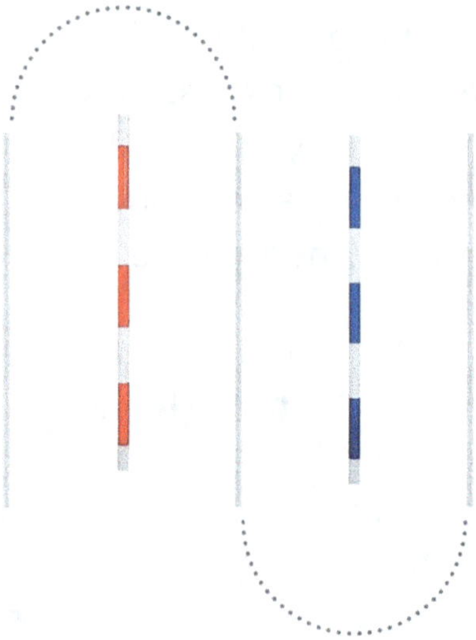

Exercise 6

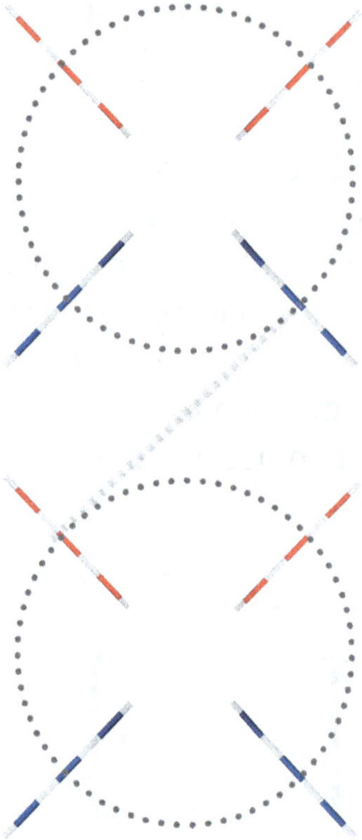

Exercise 5

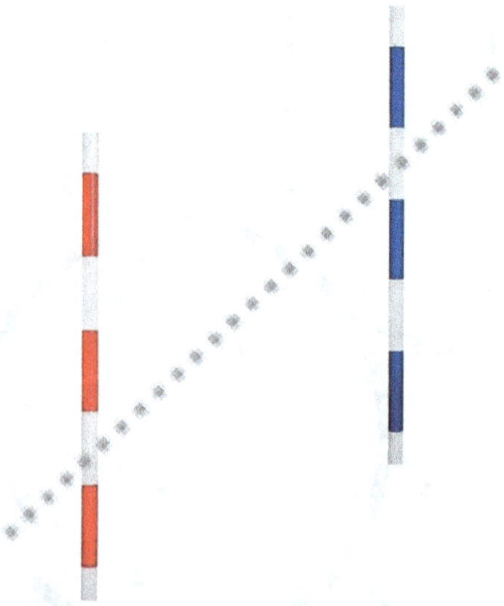

The 1 pole challenge

- Try the one pole challenge. Can you get to the point where your horse stands happily with both right hooves on one side of the pole, and the left hooves on the other? You might need to build this up in gradual stages if your horse finds it hard to understand. Reward them for the smallest try. Be happy if one hoof ends up in the right place at first and build from there. Being able to ask for a soft backup in hand really helps with this exercise.
- Walk over two poles with your horses right foot first each time.
- Make a path with two poles. Ask your horse to walk backwards through the two poles.
- Put 3 poles on the ground, one after the other. Ask your horse to walk over the centre of these poles. Then ask your horse to trot over the centre of these poles.

WALKING IN HAND

Walking in hand is great for developing the partnership between you and your horse. Think about keeping everything relaxed, having no pressure in the rope and taking your time.

EXERCISES FOR YOU

1. Walk beside your horse's shoulder with you on the near (normal) side, with a loose lead rope for 100 steps.
2. Walk beside your horse's shoulder with you on the near (normal) side, with a loose lead rope while walking a circle to the left.
3. Walk beside your horse's shoulder with you on the near (normal) side, with a loose lead rope while walking a circle to the right.
4. Walk beside your horse's shoulder with you on the off side, with a loose lead rope for 100 steps.
5. Walk beside your horse's shoulder with you on the off side, with a loose lead rope while walking a circle to the left.
6. Walk beside your horse's shoulder with you on the off side, with a loose lead rope while walking a circle to the right.

OBSTACLES

One your horse is walking nicely with you, when they are staying mentally and physically close, try some more unusual obstacles to build bravery and confidence.

FUN IDEAS

- Ask your horse to walk through a puddle.
- Ask your horse to walk over a tarpaulin.

- Open a gate and let your horse go through ahead of you. Raise the hand holding your rope and see if you can have your horse turn to face you on the other side of the gate. Then send your horse back through the gate in the other direction.
- First - save some plastic water bottles and containers. Then put 4 poles on the ground and put the bottles and containers on the ground inside them. Ask your horse to walk over the poles in different directions, walking through the plastic. Can your horse also back over the poles and through?

BONDING CHALLENGES

- Groom your horse while he is loose in the paddock.
- While your horse is loose, mirror their movements. When they move, you move. When they stop you stop.
- See if your horse will walk with you at liberty in the paddock or arena. If they will, see what happens if you put your arm out in front of you and walk towards their shoulder, will they turn away from you and keep walking? What happens if you step back a little bit towards their hind end? Do they turn towards you? This is the start of liberty work.

RIDING HORSES

Riding horses is great fun! Most of us who love horses would like to ride them and it's an amazing thing to do. Let's talk about some of the things that are important to know.

WHAT TO WEAR

- You will need riding boots or stout shoes with a heel that will stop your foot going right through the stirrups.
- A proper riding helmet or hat.
- Jodhpurs or breeches or some similar trousers that give you room to bend your legs.
- High visibility clothing if you are going out for a ride.

GETTING STARTED

The best way to start learning to ride is to get some lessons from a good instructor or go to a riding school. They should talk you through everything you need to know and give you confidence.

Here are some of my top tips:

- Use a mounting block to get on. You will probably be taught how to mount from the ground as well, but using a block whenever you can is better for the horse's back.
- Relax and let your legs sink down around the horse. Try to keep your heels down and your toes pointing forward.
- At first you will be on a lead rein to be safe. This is a good time to develop your balance and learn the basics. Your instructor will give you exercises to help you to be balanced and confident. You might be lifting your arms up while riding, maybe moving them about, even touching your toes!
- Look up and ahead towards where you are going. This is really important to let your horse know what direction to go in.
- Hold your reins softly. You need to feel the connection between your hands and your horse, but your hands can be relaxed, they don't need to be fists.
- Think about not using your reins for balance. If you pull hard on the reins it can hurt the horse's mouth. If you lose your balance you can put a hand on the front of the saddle to help yourself.
- Smile and don't forget to breathe!

NEXT STEPS

As you get more experienced you will find all sorts of things that you can try with your horse. Here are some of them:

- When you want your horse to slow down or stop - try and see how little it can take. Try just feeling relaxed in your body, letting your weight come down in the saddle a bit and breathing out. Your horse might surprise you! If your horse gets a bit faster than you want, see how they respond to you rubbing their neck just in front of the saddle as you ride and talking to them.
- Find out how little it takes your horse to turn. Ride along in a straight line and turn your head to look where you want to turn to. Don't touch the reins until you have found out if your horse can turn from just the direction that you look in. If you need to use the rein, do it gently and gradually.
- As you ride, feel how your horse moves under you. Your hips will move side to side and you will feel your horse's barrel pressing against first one of your legs then the other. This tells you which hoof is leaving the ground! You can think of this as the barrel swinging out of the way of the hoof as it leaves the ground. This means that when the right hind hoof is leaving the ground to step forward you will feel the barrel press against your left leg. See if you can get to the point where you can call out which hoof is leaving the ground as you ride! Get a friend to watch and check that you are right.

BE PATIENT

Riding can be difficult at times, but don't give up! Practise makes perfect. If you don't manage to trot very well the first time it doesn't matter - the more you try the easier it will become.

It takes hundreds of hours to learn to ride a horse well. Sometimes parents, friends, or maybe your trainer might want you to go faster than you want to. It's ok to go slowly. Because going slow is a great way to stay safe, be patient and keep you and your horse safe. So progressing at your own speed, and always having fun is the best option!

HORSES DON'T CARE ABOUT COMPETITIONS

Sometimes children and young people can be really tough on their horses. It might be because they want to win in competitions. Or maybe their parents and others really want them to win. It might be because they feel they have to impress someone. This can cause some difficult times for their horses.

You might see horses being ridden harshly, kicked hard and pulled around with the reins. You might see people losing their temper with horses. That is no fun for anyone. I think that competitions should be something that we and our horses enjoy. The most important thing isn't winning, the important thing is to take part in a way that is kind to our horses.

Decide that you want to be a kind rider and follow your own path. The most important thing is that you and your horse are happy.

Finally, congratulate yourself on every small thing you learn. Praise your horse often. Horses are amazing for allowing us to ride them, so it's our job to be as kind and patient with them as possible.

Because by listening to the horse in every situation and putting the horse's needs first, and learning as much as possible, we can become great horsemen and horsewomen that our horses love and appreciate very much.

FUN ACTIVITIES YOU CAN DO WHEN RIDING

You tried some of these activities with your horse on the ground, so they will be familiar. Now see how that work has helped both of you when you ride. Before you start with your horse - pretend to be a horse

- **The Pretend Horse Exercise :** Find a friend who can help you with this exercise. You will also need a bridle with a bit. You can hold the bit in your hands and start walking. Your friend can walk behind you holding the reins. Their job is to ask you to walk forwards, stop, turn right and left and walk backwards, without speaking. Have fun and see what it feels like. Then you can swap and your friend can hold the bit and you can hold the reins.

POLEWORK EXERCISES

As you ride the polework exercises, think about turning your horse without pulling on the reins. Keep your head up and look where you are going. See how little pressure it takes from your legs and on the reins for your horse to do what you ask.

Exercise 1: Put a wooden pole on the ground (it can be a jump pole, but even a broom handle would work). Ride towards it and see if you can choose which front hoof goes over the pole first.

THE 1 POLE CHALLENGE

Exercise 2: Do the one pole challenge. Can you get to the point where your horse stands happily with both right hooves on one side of the pole, and the left hooves on the other? Just as when you were on the ground, you might need to build this up in gradual stages if your horse finds it hard to understand. Reward them for the smallest try. Be happy if one hoof ends up in the right place at first and build from there. Being able to ask for a soft backup in hand really helps with this exercise. This exercise usually takes a few days to complete so be patient with your horse.

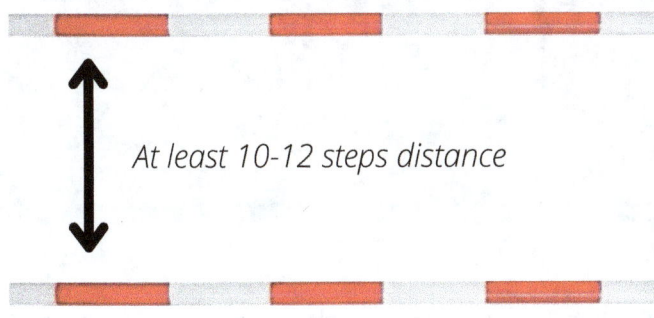

At least 10-12 steps distance

Exercise 3: Walk over two poles with your horse's right foot first each time.

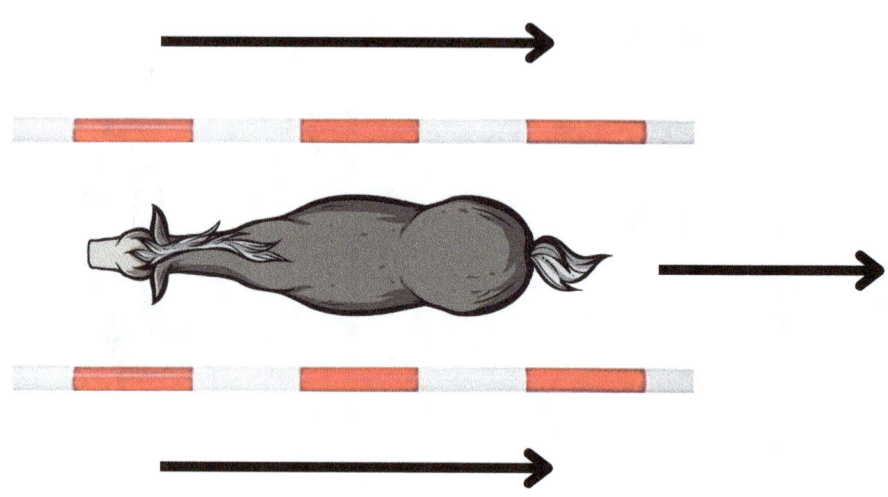

Exercise 4: Make a path with two poles. Ask your horse to walk backwards through the two poles.

Exercise 5: Put 3 or 4 poles on the ground, one after the other. Ask your horse to walk over the centre of these poles. Then ask your horse to trot over the centre of these poles. Remember to look where you are going. Don't look down!

Exercise 6: Use 4 poles to make an L shape and walk your horse through them without touching the poles. Ride a circle of about 10 metres to turn, then go back through in the other direction. When you've got that see if you can do the same... but backing up.

Exercise 7: Set up the Christmas Tree polework challenge and find at least five different ways to ride through it.

OBSTACLES

Remember the obstacles you worked on? Set them up again then get your horse and mount up.

- Ask your horse to walk through a puddle.
- Ask your horse to walk over a tarpaulin.
- Can you open a safe gate and ride your horse through without getting off? You can practise this in an arena using two jump poles, with a piece of rope between them. Use a jump cup to stop the rope falling to the bottom, then tie loops at each end and hook it over the poles. You can use this to practise riding through jumps that fasten on the right or the left, and in both directions.
- With the poles on the ground and the plastic containers - ask your horse to walk over the poles in different directions, walking through the plastic. Can your horse also back over the poles and through?

With a really good rider, no one can actually see what they are doing, or how they are asking their horse to do things. So let's try some more fun games to help you improve your riding skills!

FEEL, TIMING & BALANCE

Being a good horse person is not about asking your horse to do certain things you want to accomplish. It's also about:

- Never calling a horse disrespectful or naughty. Horses are honest. But we can confuse them when we ask them new things.
- Asking your horse the right question at the right time.
- Asking with a small cue, and not shouting at your horse or kicking them with your legs if you are riding, and never losing your temper or feeling angry.
- Stop asking the *second* your horse is thinking of the right answer. Often this can be before they even move a step! Ask how you can 'help' your horse, and not 'make' your horse do things.

RIDING SKILLS

- Ride 1 circle without looking down even once
- Can you ask your horse to go faster by just thinking about it & looking where you want to go
- Can you ask your horse to go slower by relaxing & slowing down your body and doing a big sigh, and see if your horse slows down too?
- Can you ask your horse to turn right, without using the reins and only by looking to the right?
- Can you ask your horse to turn left, without using the reins and only by looking to the left?
- Ride a figure of 8 while smiling & breathing regularly the whole time.
- Ask your horse to turn both right and left by asking on one side while giving room on the other so that they can easily turn their head.
- Don't pull on reins. You will need to never hurt the horse's mouth. You want gentle hands. Ride a square without pulling on the reins once.
- Walk your horse forward for 10 steps. Halt and back them up 10 steps. Walk them forward for 9 steps. Halt and back them up for 9 steps. Carry on until you are going forward and back for just 1 step. Can you then just rock your horse backward and forward without them taking a step? When you do this exercise make sure you don't pull on the reins. Your horse needs to know how to back up before you start.

COLLECTION

Horses weren't designed to have a human sitting on their back. When we ride our horse, our body weight is mainly added to their front legs. This extra weight the horse has to carry, can lead to serious health issues like kissing spines, back issues, joint problems, feet issues and early retirement.

When we ride our horses it's very important that we teach them good posture habits. We do not want them to carry so much extra weight on their two front legs!

As horse riders, we need to help our horses to carry us in the most healthy way possible. We do this by teaching our horse how to collect.

Collection is when the horse transfers some weight from its two front legs to its two hind legs. This helps our horse to become more athletic and powerful. Like an amazing athlete! When you teach your horse to transfer some weight to its hind legs - both in groundwork and while you are riding - it really helps improve your horse's posture and their long term health.

Let's think about the horse's body:

- The horse's hindquarters are designed to carry weight. There are a lot more flexible pieces in the hind legs, than in the front legs. So we are setting them up to be able to carry themselves in a better way.

- When the horse's balance shifts more to the hindquarters their back stops hollowing out, making it easier to carry a rider's weight with less potential to cause back issues for your horse.
- When we teach our horses collection, it helps them to become more athletic and physically powerful. If you look at any of the old paintings of people riding horses in war, They have a lot of weight on their hindquarters, their backs are rounded, their neck and head position is a natural result of the weight on their hindquarters. It is not created by riders pulling on their reins. Quite often in those old pictures the reins actually have slack in them! During these times the horse was the ultimate athlete - ready to jump, gallop and go sideways at a split second's notice, to avoid death on the battlefield and to stay safe from the enemy.

Sometimes people get confused about how to start collection. Some horse riders and instructors think they need to pull on the horse's head and ask the horse to tuck in his nose, or lower it's head a lot. *In fact, it's none of those things!*

Unfortunately some people even start tying horses' heads down with gadgets they got from the tack store. This is *very bad* for your horse's posture & health.

Remember - collection is not about the horse's head. Collection is the transfer of weight from the forequarters to the hindquarters.

We achieve this by teaching our horses to step one hind foot at a time, more deeply under his body. The best exercise for this - and the first exercise you should do when you are ready to improve your horse's posture - is shoulder in and shoulder out.

SHOULDER OUT & IN

Elaine Heney & Ozzie riding shoulder out.

Shoulder in is a movement that we can ask the horse to perform both on the ground and when we are riding them. It involves asking the horse to move both forwards and sideways at the same time, with a specific posture. Shoulder out is the mirror image of shoulder in.

- Did you know - you can do shoulder out and in using groundwork! After you and your horse are used to doing this on the ground, then you can repeat them when you are riding.
- You can start to teach them to your horse in just five minutes!
- Any horse over 3 years of age can be taught to do shoulder in and out. You do not need any special type/breed of horse to start teaching shoulder out and in.

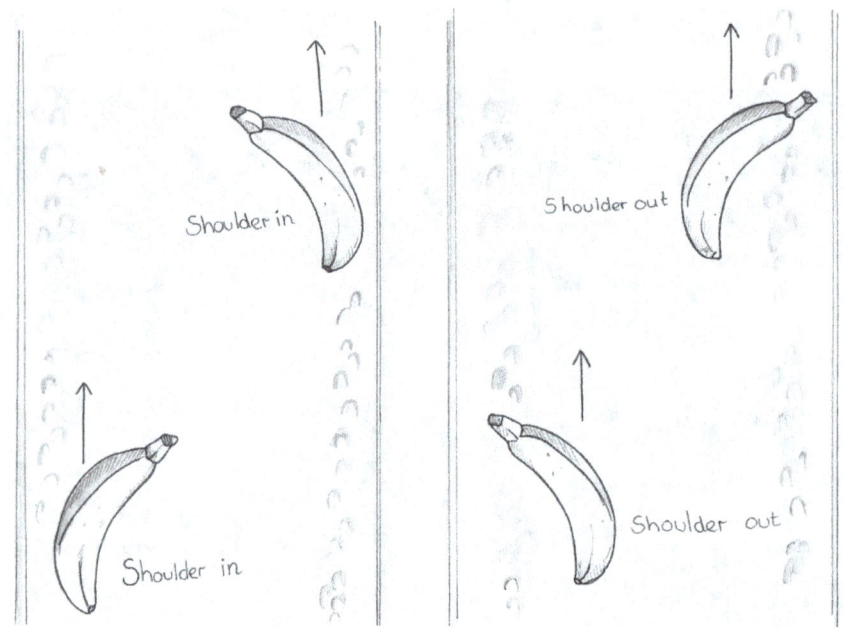

Imagine the tip of the banana is your horse's head. In shoulder out, your horse is looking slightly to the outside of the arena. In shoulder in, your horse is looking to the inside of the arena.

HOW TO START SHOULDER OUT

I like to start these exercises on the ground with the horse. I find it's the easiest way for both the human and horse to understand and learn. There are a few things to bear in mind:

- The whole horse's body will have a gentle bend through it.
- With shoulder out, the horse's head is closer to the outside of the arena.
- With shoulder out, the horse's hindquarters are closer to the inside of the arena.

- When a horse walks normally towards you his legs are on two tracks, his hind feet generally follow the direction of the front feet. When doing shoulder out (and shoulder in) your horse's feet will be on three or even four tracks, depending on how much bend is in his body. Both of these are useful for different training purposes.

Equipment and setup:

- A fenceline.
- A halter or headcollar.
- A lead rope that is at least 12 ft in length (a short lead rope won't work).
- If you have nothing else you can try with a longer lunge line or a 22ft line, but carrying a longer rope like this can be a bit difficult to handle.
- A horse who is happy with your patting and rubbing their hindquarters. If your horse gets worried when someone is near their hindquarters, or is very spooky, nervous or kicks, you are not ready to do this exercise. Instead you need to go back to basics to build confidence and relaxation instead.

Instructions:

- Walk along the fence line with your horse in hand.
- You are walking between your horse and the fence.
- Allow the lead rope to get longer and your horse to walk slightly ahead of you.
- Walk a little more towards their ribs to ask the hindquarters to move away from the fence line.
- All you want is a step or two to begin with, then walk on forwards normally again.
- Praise your horse and tell them they are wonderful!

COMMON MISTAKES TO AVOID WHEN TEACHING YOUR HORSE COLLECTION

- Asking your horse to put his nose behind the vertical (tucking his nose into his chest)
- Riding your horse with his poll below withers. This is often something taught to certain breeds of horses, like western horses. As each horse has a different conformation, your horse's natural head carriage may be when the poll at the highest point (quite common) or close to the highest point on his body. When a horse transfers weight from the forequarter to the hindquarters, the withers will naturally lift and so will the head and neck, and the horse's back will round. Low head sets may be required for certain competitions, but that does not mean this is a good idea for your horse's health.
- Using leather straps or gadgets to make horses head go lower or make horse go behind vertical
- Thinking you need to pull on reins to achieve collection. This is a really common mistake. In fact it's the hindquarters you need to think about, not the horse's head! So don't pull on your horse's mouth!
- Forgetting to teach your horse the shoulder in and out exercises. Teaching shoulder in and out is the correct way to teach your horse's body to step the hind end under more deeply. This in turn causes a weight shift to the hindquarters, a rounded back, lifted withers and an athletic and healthy horse to ride.

GOOD HORSEMANSHIP

Good horsemanship doesn't mean you have to be the best rider or trainer. **It does mean considering your horse's feelings every time you are with him.**

When you are learning to ride try to always remember that a horse can feel a fly landing on his back, so he can feel everything you do. It's really hard to learn a new skill and be gentle at the same time, but you need to try.

When you want to go faster, instead of suddenly kicking your horse hard, try *thinking* of moving faster first, and increasing the energy you are feeling in your body.

Imagine the ice cream shop is giving away free ice cream! Feel that excitement in your body, and your horse will feel it too.

If that isn't enough, then try a gentle nudge with your legs. **Then, as soon as your horse does move faster, stop asking!** Horses know they have done the right thing when you stop asking. Always remember to thank your horse too.

FINALLY...

According to the Guiness Book of Records the oldest horse ever was Old Billy, who was born in Lancashire in 1760 and died at 62 years old in 1822!

The most important thing about owning horses and being around them is that it should be fun. Don't be hard on yourself or on your horse. It takes hundreds of hours to learn to ride a horse well and it takes hundreds of hours for horses to learn to be amazing to ride. It doesn't matter if a friend can do a rising trot (also known as posting) after only two lessons and you are still having problems after five. It will come, it's OK if it takes a bit longer! Your horse doesn't care.

Sometimes you might feel as if you should be doing more with your horse. Sometimes people you talk to will think you should be doing more as well. You should be jumping higher, going faster, competing... Horses don't care about running faster, jumping higher or going to competitions. They like to feel safe and relaxed. Your goal is to be the best friend for your horse that you can be. Be kind, be patient, care for him when he is sick and listen to him when he is talking to you.

GLOSSARY OF TERMS

- Foal - a foal is a baby horse, up to a year old.
- Colt - a colt is a young male horse up to four years old.
- Filly - a filly is a young female horse up to four years old.
- Mare - a mare is a female horse that is four years old or over.
- Stallion - a stallion is a male horse who is able to father foals.
- Gelding - a gelding is a male horse who has had an operation so that he can't father foals.
- Walk - The walk is the slowest gait or speed that a horse moves at. It is called a "4 beat gait" because when a horse is walking each hoof hits the ground independently.
- Trot - The trot is sometimes also called the "jog". It is faster than the walk and is a "2 beat gait". The hooves hit the ground together in diagonal pairs - this means that the front left and rear hind legs move forward and back together as a pair.
- Canter - The canter is sometimes also called the "lope". It is faster than a trot and called a "3 beat gait". In the canter the horse will be on either the right or left lead. When the horse is on the right lead the left hind, right hind and left front leave the ground at the same time, followed by the right front. On the left lead the right hind, left hind and right front leave the ground at the same time, followed by the left front. When you are cantering in circles you will usually want your horse to take the right lead when circling right, and the left lead when circling left.

GLOSSARY OF TERMS

- Gallop - The gallop is faster than the canter. In the gallop the hooves hit the ground one at a time. During the gallop there is a period of suspension when all four hooves have left the ground at the same time. The faster the horse is going the longer the period of suspension is.
- Other gaits - Some horses have more than the four gaits - walk, trot, canter and gallop. You will likely hear about them as you learn more about horses. For example, pacers move very fast at what looks like a trot, with the legs on each side moving together. There are other horses, such as Paso Fino horses, who can move with each hoof hitting the ground individually - one at a time - which makes them very comfortable to ride. Icelandic horses have a gait called the tolt.

Congratulations! You are on your way to becoming an amazing horse person. I would be very grateful if you could share your review & a picture of this book online. Thank you.

LESSONS I LEARNED FROM THIS BOOK:

_____
_____
_____
_____
_____
_____
_____
_____
_____
_____

Saddlestone
Connemara Pony Listening School

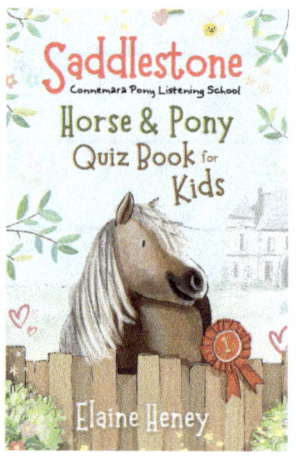

by #1 best-selling author

Elaine Heney

THE CONNEMARA ADVENTURE SERIES FOR KIDS 8+

www.writtenbyelaine.com

HORSE BOOKS
by #1 best-selling author
ELAINE HENEY

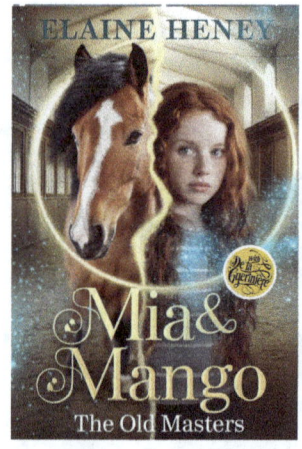

www.elaineheneybooks.com

www.ingramcontent.com/pod-product-compliance
Lightning Source LLC
Chambersburg PA
CBHW060043230426
43661CB00004B/639